BLESSED ARE THE POOR

RHONDA CALHOUN

HEART
Publishing

Heart Publishing
PMB 177 12905 South 71 Hwy.
Grandview, MO 64030
harvesthome@juno.com

All Scripture quotations, unless otherwise indicated, are taken from the New
American Standard Bible. Copyright © 1960, 1962, 1963, 1971, 1972, 1973,
1975, 1977 by the Lockman Foundation. Used by permission.
(www.Lockman.org)

Edited by Jackie MacGirvin and Lynn Kohout
Printed in the United States of America
Library of Congress Cataloging-in-Publication Data Card Number

Calhoun, Rhonda Lee, 1957-
Blessed Are the Poor/Rhonda Lee Calhoun
p. cm.
ISBN 0-9704791-2-3 (pbk.)
1. Poor-United States. 1. Title.

HC110.P6 C25 2001
305.5'69'0973-dc21

2001026486

Dedication

𝕿his book is dedicated to my wonderful heavenly Father who has always loved and cared for me. Without Him, this book would certainly have never been written. And, to my wonderful husband, Danny, who is the greatest servant I know.

Acknowledgements

To my oldest daughter, Misty, who was my faithful cheerleader, always there with encouragement. To my daughter, Dana, who read and reread each chapter offering insight and suggestions. To my dear friends, Jackie MacGirvin and Lynn Kohout who graciously spent countless hours editing this manuscript.

Thank you all for loving and believing in me.

Contents

Foreword

Part of God's plan for our lives is to teach us through experiences, many of which are filled with hardships that help to shape our future. Rhonda Calhoun is one of those whose childhood was enormously difficult. She came from a background of poverty and abuse but God has used those experiences to accomplish much good. The Lord has graciously given her a wonderful ministry serving the poor and hurting.

Rhonda, her husband Danny, and their two daughters, Misty and Dana, moved to Kansas City from Georgia in 1993. They came into my life on a hot August day in the parking lot of Metro Christian Fellowship in Grandview, Missouri. From that first meeting, we locked arms and hearts in friendship and service.

Rhonda is a dreamer; she's a passionate pursuer of God's heart. She's a woman of prayer who has focused her life on serving those of little account, those who have no recognition, those who the world often sees as unimportant: the children, the elderly, the sick, and the hurting. She's a woman who has risen above the pain in her own life and has received healing by extending her loving hands to others.

In 1995, Rhonda and Danny started Harvest Home. Through

this ministry the Lord has sent many volunteers to serve those who the world has forgotten. They organized Kid's and Youth Explosions, which are gatherings in low-income areas, where children and young people come together to play, to be loved, and to hear God's word. They also fed and befriended the homeless weekly. Rain or shine, Rhonda's arms have been extended to the needy. In addition, she has ministered in nursing homes, hospitals and churches. Literally, hundreds of lives have been changed by the love of God that's been transferred through Rhonda's arms into the Kansas City community.

Out of Rhonda's love for the Lord and His people, she's brought hope, the blessed hope of Jesus to others. Her actions have built faith among the volunteers, and in all those who have seen what the love of God can do in people's lives. The fruit of Rhonda's ministry is obvious in her life, in the life of her family, her church, and among the poor.

Rhonda and Danny's efforts through Harvest Home had a major impact in their local church, Metro Christian Fellowship. The Calhoun's were pioneers in bringing a desire to the hearts of their church to minister to the poor and since then other ministries have been birthed. Now, through this book, Rhonda's love is moving beyond Kansas City and her local church, to share her heart with the world.

This book is an inspiration to all that have a desire to see God's love in action, for it's a book about love. I am confident you will enjoy these real life stories. Rhonda and her army of volunteers are ordinary people who have done extraordinary things. To those who have been faithful in the little things, we say, *"Well done."*

Enjoy, for this book is filled with apples of gold from the Father's heart!

— **Les Woller**

And turning His gaze on His disciples, He began to say, *"Blessed are you who are poor, for yours is the kingdom of God."*

Luke 6:20

Introduction

There are those who have no voice. No one hears their cries. No one knows their pain. People surround them but no one sees them. They are the poor. Poor financially, but oftentimes rich in other ways. Yet, there is One who hears their cries and sees every injustice. He passionately loves them and desperately cares about every detail of their lives. *Nothing* escapes His watchful eye.

Often, we look at their situations and decide all is hopeless. We understand that a miracle is needed to deliver them from their impossible circumstances. Miracles are birthed out of the rich soil of compassionate hearts, out of hearts willing to listen and respond to their cries. In these broken lives, God's unconditional love can easily be demonstrated in practical ways. God's love truly is the greatest gift we have to give. And in giving, **we** encounter Jesus and **we** are changed.

Come with me on a journey of miracles. A journey that begins in a small rural town, moves to the suburbs, then continues to the inner city. A journey that involves real people just like you and me. A journey of friendships, tears, laughter, and pain. This is a journey where miracles really do happen and lives really do change.

Part I

IN THE BEGINNING

SAFE IN HIS ARMS

When all around me crumbles and falls,
And my dreams lie crushed at my feet,
When life is frightening and love can't be found,
I am safe in His arms.

When the world is empty and dark,
And I can't see beyond the pain,
When my strength and my heart fails within me,
I am safe in His arms.

When the night is long and lonely,
And hope is nowhere to be found,
When suffering surrounds me on every side,
I am still safe in His arms.

When the day of destruction comes
And floods rage against our very souls,
When life, as we know it, comes to an end,
We will run to Him and we will be
Forever—safe in His arms.

— Rhonda

Chapter One

Safe In His Arms

And those who are most helpless will eat,
And the needy will lie down in security.
Isaiah 14:30

Life, love, peace and trust
Each of these are strange to us.
Sure we live and love, but do we know
What life really has to show?
— Rhonda, age 12

It was late summer of 1964 in southern Georgia. On the outskirts of a small, rural town, a mother sat in silence in an old, unkempt farmhouse. Carefully propping her broken ankle on a rickety footstool, she wondered how she was going to feed her four young children. Scenes from the car accident two nights before plagued her weary mind and body. Her husband was driving drunk — again. She and her four children were in the car, but miraculously no one was killed.

Her husband will be in the hospital a few days and then what? His employer did call, but this time to fire him. Their only car was destroyed and as usual, they have no money. The kitchen shelves were bare and the refrigerator was almost empty. Depression was close at hand and she knew it. Reaching for her bible, she reminded herself of the one thing no one—not even her husband could take from her—an unwavering faith in a God who had sustained her to this day and would most certainly continue to do so. Hadn't the officer called that very morning to tell her how God Himself had protected them?

He said, *"Good morning. This is officer Smith. I know you don't remember me, but I was the first officer to arrive at your accident. I just wanted to call and let you know that I believe it's a miracle y'all are alive. I've worked many accidents and when I walked up to your car my stomach sank. From its condition, I was certain I wouldn't find any survivors. You can't imagine my amazement when I discovered that not only were y'all alive, but you had only minor injuries. After writing my report, I'm even more convinced the whole thing isn't just one miracle, but several rolled into one. The fact your car flew through that pecan orchard without hitting a tree is the first miracle. To think that your car just 'happened' to land on a mound of gravel ten feet in diameter is equally amazing. If that's not enough, I learned that a department of transportation truck had mechanical problems that morning and was instructed to unload its truckload of gravel in the place where your car landed. The fact that your car landed upside-down on that gravel instead of on the hard ground saved your lives. The whole thing was a series of events that only God Himself could've orchestrated. In my book, that's a miracle."*

She looked up from her handkerchief, which she'd folded and unfolded countless times. Three of her four children were sitting on the floor in front of an old fan, which struggled to circulate the hot air through this poorly furnished room. A definite, almost tangible sadness filled the air. The room itself appeared to be clothed with despair, its once white walls were very dingy and dark. Homemade curtains hung limply over the windows, occasionally moving as a breath of hot air lifted them from their lifeless state. The old, green carpet was worn thin in so many places that the underlying floorboards were clearly visible. Numerous houseplants in Crisco tins and margarine bowls were scattered around the room, adding the only hint of life to this otherwise dreary room.

Across the hall, I laid curled up on my bed staring out the window. My long, dark hair was tangled and my skinny, seven-year-old body was bruised from more than just the car accident. I looked into the heavens, which stretched out endlessly before me. The night sky was alive with thousands upon thousands of stars dancing to a silent song. Oh, how I longed to see beyond the stars and into heaven's gate, for somewhere out there was my heavenly Father!

Picking up my doll, Tabitha, I gently placed her in the windowsill and whispered, *"Everything's going to be all right, you'll see. God loves us and He'll take care of us. And one day, we'll live with Him in heaven; then we'll never cry again and that's a promise."*

Kissing Tabitha's cheek, I thought back to the first time I saw my precious doll. My brother and I had been digging through the dump behind our house looking for anything that might be useful, when I noticed a tiny hand poking through the pile of refuse. Could it possibly be? Quickly, I dug through the garbage to uncover a very dirty and nearly baldheaded doll. Brushing the filth from her face, I saw that most of her eyelashes were gone and ink scribbles covered her cheeks and forehead. But that didn't matter to me. To me she was the most beautiful doll in the whole world. I couldn't believe my fortune; I'd prayed for a doll many times and now I had one! I held her tightly and ran all the way home—I wasn't about to risk losing my newly found treasure.

I ran in the back door and went directly to the bathroom. With the sink full of soapy water, I scrubbed as gently as possible, being careful not to get any soap in her eyes. Realizing the ink was there to stay, I whispered, *"It's okay. I know just how you feel; I'm not pretty either. But don't be sad. I think you're beautiful just like you are. And don't you worry, I promise to never throw you away. I'm going to love you. I'll call you Tabitha, cause Tabitha is the prettiest name I know."*

God and Tabitha were my only friends. At school, my classmates, when they weren't busy making fun of me just avoided me. My obvious poverty made me an interesting topic most days. In my pain and loneliness, I turned to God for the companionship I craved. The fact that I couldn't see God or touch Him didn't change the fact that He was real. God was just as real to me as the invisible, untouchable air I breathed and just as necessary.

My earthly father was an alcoholic and quite abusive. I suffered much at his hand. God, in His great love, revealed Himself to me in such a way that I clearly understood He wasn't anything like my earthly father. God alone was good and perfect. And because I saw Him as such, I held Him in the highest regard. I always approached Him with the utmost respect and at the same time, talked to Him as one would a best friend. I told Him everything, every detail of my day, both the good and the bad. My Father proved Himself to be compassionate and gentle. Not once did I go to Him with my pain and sorrow that I didn't leave His presence comforted and filled with His love. He was the love of my life.

And so it was, for probably the hundredth time, I pressed my face against the torn screen and poured out my heart to heaven:

Dear God,

I know you saw our wreck and I'm glad you did cause we really needed your help. Boy, was I scared! Dad was driving real fast and every time momma asked him to slow down, he'd just go faster. Momma said he was going over 100 mph. She begged him to let her drive, but he just cussed a lot, then said, 'If you think this is fast, what do you think about this?'

Then, the car sounded like it got mad. Momma grabbed the baby and yelled, 'Oh, God help us—we're going off the bridge!'

Well, we didn't go over the bridge, but the car did fly off the road. We busted through a fence and the car did somersaults in the air between these great big trees. We didn't even hit one—I know that's cause You were there. Anyway, we landed upside-down on a big pile of gravel.

I woke up and it was so dark and quiet that I thought I was dead. I tried to move, but couldn't. My hand was caught in the window and was hurtin' real bad. That's when I figured out I wasn't dead cause nuthin' hurts in heaven.

It wasn't long before I heard my baby sister crying, but couldn't see her. I couldn't see anything cause it was so dark. I called for help, but nobody came. Then, I heard my dad. He was outside the car talking to his momma. That scared me too cause his momma died when he was a little boy, so how could he be talking to her?

Finally, I heard my momma's voice; she was somewhere in the car. She told me to keep calling, so she could find me. She had to crawl on her belly cause the car was squished flat. It seemed like it took her such a long time. Momma told me she'd been trying to get the baby out, but couldn't cause she was stuck tight. Momma worked real hard to get my hand out, but the window wouldn't open and she couldn't break it no matter how hard she tried. After a while, she left and I was alone again in the dark. Gas was pouring all around me and the smell burned my nose and throat. I was praying so hard that dad wouldn't light a cigarette.

After a real long time, momma crawled back to me and said she'd gotten the baby out and she'd get me out too. She'd tried to find something to pry the window open with, but there wasn't anything. I kept pushing the power button, but it was broke. Momma said that's cause the engine was turned off. I thought I was going to be stuck in that car forever. Momma said for me to pull as hard as I could, even if it hurt. She pried the window down with her fingers and I pulled. She was real strong and I pulled real hard and my fingers came out. We crawled out as fast as we could, but that wasn't very fast cause there wasn't much room.

It was just as dark outside as it was in the car. My brother and sister were walking in circles, looking for a shoe that was lost. A stranger was holding my baby sister who was crying. My dad was sitting on the ground still talking to his momma. He had blood all over his face and that really scared me. My momma tried to walk to the baby but fell down screaming. That's cause her ankle was broken.

I was so cold. I stuck my hands in my pockets and they were full of broken glass. My ears, hair and socks even had glass in them. My clothes were wet from the gas; I was very sleepy, so I laid on the ground and waited.

It was such a long time before I heard the wonderful siren. The warm, flashing lights made me feel better. The next thing I knew, a man in a very white shirt was standing over me. He reached down and picked me up. I thought he was an angel and was taking me to heaven to live with You, but sadly, he was just a man.

As he carried me to the ambulance, he said, "Little lady, God must really love you. He put the whole world on hold tonight, just so He could keep you safe in His arms."

I couldn't believe he called me 'little lady'. I've been called a lot of names, but never a nice name like that. Would You do something really special for that man cause he was so nice to me?

Anyway, that's how momma got a broken ankle. Dad's in the hospital and we don't have any money for anything. Our food is almost gone, again. I know we're a lot of work, but You're all we've got and we sure do need Your help. Amen.

I buried my face in Tabitha's cotton belly and cried the tears I'd been holding back since the accident. My Father in heaven heard my cries and groaned—all of heaven stood at attention. My Father groaned because of His great love for me. He felt my suffering in the very depths of His being. He motioned for three angels to draw near. Without hesitating, they knelt before the great throne. Leaning forward, my Father said, *"Go and love her with My love."* With a nod, they left for earth. My Father looked down and whispered, *"Help is on its way, little one."*

Instantly, the angels arrived to comfort this little child of the King. A sweet peace filled my weary frame. With this loving touch came the familiar ache that I'd had for as long as I could remember—a deep intense longing to be held in the arms of my heavenly Father. Oh, how I longed for Him! Pressing my face against the screen again, I whispered, *"God, I know why the stars are so happy—it's because they are so close to You."*

Once more, tears filled my eyes. *"I wish I lived up there with You, then I'd be happy, too."*

Suddenly, my conversation was interrupted by a knock on the front door. I wiped the tears on my sleeve, placed Tabitha comfortably on my pillow, and hurried to see who this rare visitor might be. Standing in the dim porch light was Mr. and Mrs. Brook, a couple from my church. In their arms were numerous bags filled with groceries. Several trips were made to their car before the tremendous amount of food was inside.

Excited, I climbed on top of our homemade table as Mr. and Mrs. Brook quietly talked with my mother in the corner. I'd never seen so much food! Unable to contain my excitement, I unloaded each bag, holding each item up for my brother and sisters to see. My oldest sister, embarrassed by my exuberant demonstration, whispered for me to 'act more civilized'. Too excited to be restrained, I continued announcing each food item. At times, I had to read the labels because there was food I came across that I'd never seen before.

Finally, the last bag was empty and a mountain of food surrounded me. With tears of joy, I whispered, *"When I grow up, this is what I'm going to do. I'm going to take food to kids just like me."*

That hot summer night, I climbed into bed and as always, placed my pillow in the windowsill. The vastness of the heavens stretched endlessly before me making me acutely aware of my smallness. Just a tiny speck of a girl on a great, big planet, yet, I was noticed and loved by a huge God. *"How can this be?"* I whispered.

I struggled for words to express my adoration and appreciation. Pulling Tabitha close, I prayed, *"Dear Father, I sure am little and You sure are big and I'm so glad size doesn't matter to you.*

Thank you for loving poor, little girls like me. Thank you for sending Mr. and Mrs. Brook with all that food. And thank you for putting the whole world on hold just for me. In Jesus' name I pray— oh, I almost forgot, Tabitha and I sure do love You. Amen."

I lay in my bed and imagined my heavenly Father left His throne and traveled through time and space. He arrived in my simple room, and filled it with His wonderful light and love. Sitting on the edge of my bed, He scooped me up in His great big, wonderful arms and held me close! His glorious love filled me, as I snuggled against His heart and fell fast asleep—once more, safe in His arms.

* * * * * * * * * *

The food brought to my family that night was so much more than just food for our hungry stomachs, it was food for my aching, hungry soul. Their act of kindness helped shape my destiny. Today, I'm living out that childhood dream.

My husband and I, along with another couple, Les and Mary Lee Woller, began a ministry called Harvest Home in 1995. We reach out with food, clothing, and various other necessities to men, women and children in need. Our heart is to love, not only with words, but also in *deeds*. And in doing so, we share the message of the gospel of Jesus Christ that no one is too poor, insignificant or broken to be loved.

And it all began that summer night, so long ago, with a simple, but very powerful act of kindness.

I Long To Be

I long to be
Like one of these,
Who spend their days
In simple ways.

Oh, how I long to be
Happy, childish and free.
To be like a cool breeze
Blowing through the trees.

Or like a lazy stream;
That is my dream.
To be alone, without care
Like the clouds in the air.

To be like one of these
Would more than please
My searching, weary mind,
And rest I might find.

And then the smallest matter
Would bring about laughter.
And I'd fill the air with joy
And make a happy noise.

My eyes would be so bright,
Filled with childish delight.
My face would glow
And love I would know.

— Rhonda, age 11

Part II

THOSE WITHOUT A HOME

During the past five years working among the poor, I've met many wonderful people. It's their stories that fill the pages of this book.

Out of love and respect, I've changed many of their names.

Jesus said to him, *"The foxes have holes, and the birds of the air have nests, but the Son of Man has no where to lay His head."*

Matthew 8:20

A HOMELESS MAN

He came to us
With the heart of a servant.
He knelt down and washed our feet
Demonstrating for us greatness.

His only employment
Was to implore us to love God *and*
To love our neighbors the way we love ourselves
With no regard to social status or bank accounts.

The Son of man had no possessions,
Therefore, nothing possessed Him.
He owned neither house, nor camel, nor gold.
Yet, in reality—He owned it all.

He wasn't politically correct.
But He was definitely correct.
He never excluded anyone—not even Judas,
Calling him 'friend' to the very end.

He never complained and never looked back.
He never quit, gave in, or gave up.
And He never regretted His decision to come
Even while hanging on the cross.

The Son of God hated no one.
Not even those who nailed Him to a cross.
He loved His friends and He loved His enemies.
Not too bad—for a homeless man.

— Rhonda

"Penny giving one of her great hugs"

CHAPTER TWO

A Penny and a Prayer

Don't judge lest you be judged.
For in the way you judge, you will be judged;
And by your standard of measure, it will be measured to you.
Matthew 7:1-2

There's a hunger deep in the soul of every man,
woman and child.
A hunger cradled in the very depths of our beings,
A hunger to love and be loved.

𝕴 stepped back from the crowd of homeless people. I was surrounded by trash, broken bottles, and broken lives. Everything about this place screamed of suffering and hopelessness.

Just a few feet away, a drug deal was taking place. On the corner, a man and woman were shouting obscenities at each other as freely as if they were the only two people on earth. The park was filled with homeless people clutching their belongings to keep them safe from the ever present reality of losing them to the nearest thief.

The sun was unusually hot and there was no way to escape its blistering heat. In spite of everything, I was glad to be here and there was no place I would've rather been.

I kicked a small rock and saw what looked like a coin buried in the dirt. I quickly dug it out, brushed it off and smiled. It was a penny. Worthless—that's what most people would think. But not me, or at least, not anymore. Not since getting to know a homeless woman named Penny. Closing my hand tightly around this dirty, little copper coin, I prayed for Penny and the many others who are often thought of as worthless. I showed my friend, Mary Lee, my newly found treasure. She asked, *"I wonder how Penny is?"*

We met Penny our first night on the streets. It was November, 1995 and five fearful people drove to the inner city armed with sandwiches, hot coffee, blankets, and a strong desire to reach the homeless. None of us had ever done anything like this and had no idea what to expect. Needless to say, that week we had prayed a lot. During the thirty minute drive, we asked God to surround us with a circle of fire so nothing could harm us. We arrived at the park and suddenly, several police cars descended on the building directly across the street. Within minutes, the street behind and in front of us was barricaded. The swirling red, yellow and blue lights cast a fiery glow on the buildings around us, giving the appearance of fire encircling us. We hadn't expected such a dramatic answer to our prayers. God had heard and was letting us know it. With this demonstration, peace filled our nervous hearts and chased away our fears. In that moment, we knew there was no place on earth any safer for us than where we were right then. We resumed unloading the van, while keeping a curious eye on the police drama unfolding across the street.

As homeless men and women walked by, we offered them a hot meal and coffee. Many were fearful and kept walking. But there were a few who stopped. One was a woman who boldly walked up and asked what we were doing. We introduced ourselves and explained why we were there. She said her name was Penny, then eagerly accepted a cup of coffee, but politely refused the food. Patting her stomach she said, *"Why honey, somebody else needs that food more than I do."*

Penny looked about thirty-years-old. She wore a simple, black dress several sizes too small for her generous frame. She was in perpetual motion as she talked, trying desperately to get warm.

She had no coat or gloves and her legs were bare. The temperature was near freezing. It wasn't long before one of the volunteers removed her own gloves and hat and offered them to Penny. Surprised by this stranger's act of kindness, she hesitated and then asked, *"Are you sure?"*

Smiling she answered, *"Yeah, I'm sure."*

Penny quickly pulled the hat over her ears and slipped her frozen hands into the gloves. *"Thanks so very much."*

Penny had a wonderful personality, very friendly and outgoing. We spent most of the evening listening to her stories. It soon felt as if we were old friends. At one point, Penny stood still and quietly asked, *"Did you know I have a daughter? She lived with me for a while, but not anymore. This isn't a good place for a child, so I took her to live with one of my relatives. She's giving her a good Christian upbringing. I want her to have a better life than this. She deserves so much more than I can give her."*

Tears filled Penny's eyes. Then, she quickly changed the subject by singing her favorite song, 'I Got You Babe'. Her voice wasn't so great, but the energy she put into it more than made up for what she lacked in talent. Our time together passed much too quickly and it was soon time to leave. Penny promised to meet us again the following Thursday and we said our good-byes.

Just as we pulled out of our parking place, the multitude of police cars did the same. I couldn't believe it! God's protection over us was obvious. He made sure we knew He had answered our prayers. Needless to say, we left that night very encouraged and *very* excited.

From then on, Penny was always waiting for us. She rarely accepted food, saying that others needed it more, but eagerly accepted our friendship. One particular night, Penny and I were in the middle of a serious conversation when her pimp walked up and demanded she come with him. She looked at me, then back at him and said, *"Are you blind or what? Can't you see that I'm spending time with my Christian friends?"*

I held my breath, fearing his reaction. To my surprise, he simply looked at her. After what seemed like an eternity, he looked at me, nodded, then walked back across the street where his other 'girls' waited. I'd heard many stories of how pimps horribly mistreat their 'girls' when they don't follow their instructions. I wondered if this would be the last time I'd see Penny. Thankfully, the next week Penny sat on the steps waiting, while her pimp was busy taking care of business across the street.

Several months passed, then an interesting thing happened. Penny's pimp came over for a cup of coffee then looked through the clothing, taking some to his girls. Two weeks later, he allowed the other girls to join us. Like a proud mother, Penny introduced the girls to us eagerly pointing out good things about each one. Over the next couple of months, we reached out in friendship to them and, oftentimes, prayed with them. These girls despised what they were doing, but were convinced there was no way out. In their minds 'once a prostitute, always a prostitute'. After all, who would ever care about a prostitute? They had no idea that Jesus loved them to the extent that He died for them.

One night Penny showed up alone, I asked where the other girls were. She answered, *"I finally stood up to my sorry, no-good-for-nothing 'keeper' and told him I wanted out. I braced myself for a good fight, but instead he just opened the door and told me to get out and never come back. So, here I am."*

Over the next two years, our friendship continued to grow and on several occasions, Penny openly shared her desire to please God. Her heart was very tender toward God. Her honesty about her sins and weaknesses really impacted me. I longed to be more like that. Many times, Penny talked about living on the streets; she cried frequently and hugged a lot. I can still feel her arms around my neck and can still hear her whisper in my ear, *"Thanks for loving me."*

Each week, at the end of our time together, we'd join hands with those who were still there and pray. I loved hearing Penny pray. She prayed simple prayers straight from her heart, almost always bringing tears to my eyes. She was beautiful, even though, she was covered in shame and guilt.

While working among the homeless, I had learned a lot about the many dangers of living on the street. Each week, I'd breathe a sigh of relief when I'd see Penny waiting in her usual place. But the day I feared eventually came when Penny wasn't there. About an hour passed, I looked up and saw Penny in the back seat of a passing car. The car slowed almost to a stop, so I yelled Penny's name and waved wildly. The car door flew open and Penny jumped out. She ran to me with arms flung wide and tears pouring down her face. Clinging to me, we walked to the church steps.

"Why are you crying, Penny?"

"When I left you guys last week, I decided I wasn't going to drink any more. I made it five whole days. Then, a so-called friend gave me a bottle of whiskey. Well, I drank it and the next thing I know, I'm drunk. I really do want to be good. I want to quit drinking and get a job. I want to raise my daughter. I want to be the one who takes her to church, the one who dresses her for school and takes her shopping. I don't want to be like this!"

From her broken heart came tears of shame and despair. She fell into me and sobbed on my shoulder, holding me so tightly, I could barely breathe. She clung to me like a drowning child, as if I was her only hope. I rocked her in my arms. There wasn't a thing I could say.

Finally she whispered, *"Do you think God hates me?"*

Tears now filled my eyes. I answered, *"No, Penny, God doesn't hate you. He loves you so very much. Unlike most people, when God sees us, He looks at our hearts. In seeing you, He loves you just as you are. But that doesn't mean He wants you to stay the way you are. What it does mean is that He wants what's best for you. He wants you to be free from those things that are harmful to you; He wants you to be free from your sins. But there's one thing you should never doubt and that's God's love for you."*

"I hate my life the way it is. I want to change, but I can't do it on my own. I know I could make it if I could be with people like you."

I looked into her dark brown eyes and saw pain-filled longing. My heart ached. I wanted to help, but what could I do? Leaning against my shoulder was a bruised, battered lamb searching, longing for safety and yearning to be healed. I wanted to take her to a place where she'd be loved and cared for, a place where she'd find hope and healing. Anguish filled my heart because I didn't know of a place like that.

After quite sometime, Penny's tears finally stopped. We sat quietly for the longest time. Eventually, I had to break the silence to tell her it was time for us to leave. *"Could we pray just one more time?"* she asked.

The homeless team formed a circle with our arms around each other. Penny was the first and the last to pray. Pulling away from the curb, I turned to wave one last time. Penny leaned against the light pole. A wave of sadness surged through my body. I felt like I was looking at a helpless lamb in the midst of a dark, evil wilderness. Oh, how I cried!

Penny was in my thoughts and prayers much more than usual that week. She was a penny that had found its way into the depths of my heart, taken root and grown into a beautiful rose, complete with thorns. She desperately needed a safe place, where she could recover from her many years of abuse. I called several churches looking for that place, but was unable to find help for her.

I was so glad when Thursday finally came and we returned to the park. But sadly, Penny wasn't waiting on the steps. Throughout the night, I anxiously looked for her, but to no avail. The next week came and there was still no Penny. In all the time we'd known her, she'd never missed two weeks in a row. We began a street campaign, asking everyone who came by if they'd seen Penny. No one had.

Then, as we were packing to leave, a man walked up and said, *"Penny was attacked a couple of weeks ago. A man stabbed her. She was cut up real bad. But I heard she's going to make it."*

With a heavy heart, I sat on the old church steps where Penny and I had spent so many hours together. I could see her face, her smile, and her tears. I could hear her singing. I thought about the last time I saw her leaning against that light pole, looking so helpless and vulnerable. Oh, how painfully true that turned out to be.

After four long weeks, our van turned the corner and I saw her. Even before we came to a complete stop, I was out the door. Penny and I hugged and cried, and hugged and cried some more. She hobbled around, repeatedly hugging our team.

We gathered on the church steps to hear what had happened. Penny said, *"A couple nights after I left you guys, a man jumped me. He beat me real bad, then cut me several times. I thought I was going to die, but I really wasn't too bummed cause I know heaven's so much better than this place. Anyway, you want to see where he cut me?"*

Before I could gracefully refuse, she discreetly lifted her skirt. On both her thighs, were numerous slashes, one of them was at least twelve inches long. Penny said, *"I know God was watching out for me or I'd be dead right now."*

Over the next six months or so, Penny would be waiting faithfully for us and then, for some unknown reason, she disappeared. Once again, we asked about her; but no one had any knowledge of her whereabouts. It's been over a year since I've seen my friend. I miss her.

In the three years of knowing Penny, I've learned much. But I think the most important thing I learned was how vital it is to love more and judge less.

Today, when I find pennies lying on the ground, I view them quite differently. In the past, I would walk over them. It was easy to do that because I didn't think a penny was worth very much. Now, I find myself actually looking for them. Since knowing Penny, I've made a commitment to pick up any abandoned coins. I use them as a reminder to pray for all the Penny's out there who are lost and hurting.

* * * * * * * *

I've found it isn't as difficult as one might think to stop and pick up a lost penny. It can be as simple as...

A hug
 A card
  A smile
   A prayer
    A greeting
     A wildflower
      A loving note
       A listening ear

A cup of coffee
A heartfelt touch
A cup of cold water
And on and on it goes
Always giving, ever growing
Never stopping, never ending.

"But when the Son of Man comes in His glory, and all the angels with Him, then He will sit on His glorious throne. All the nations will be gathered before Him; and He will separate them from one another, as the shepherd separates the sheep from the goats; and He will put the sheep on His right, and the goats on the left.

Then the King will say to those on His right, 'Come, you who are blessed of My Father, inherit the kingdom prepared for you from the foundation of the world. For I was hungry, and you gave Me something to eat; I was thirsty, and you gave Me something to drink; I was a stranger, and you invited Me in; naked, and you clothed Me; I was sick, and you visited Me; I was in prison, and you came to Me.'

Then, the righteous will answer Him, saying, 'Lord, when did we see You hungry, and feed You, or thirsty, and give You drink? And when did we see You a stranger and invite You in, or naked, and clothe You? And when did we see You sick, or in prison, and come to You?'

The King will answer and say to them, 'Truly I say to you, to the extent that you did it to one of these brothers of Mine, even the least of them, you did it to Me.'"

Matthew 25:31-40

CHAPTER THREE

Stone Steps

There is no fear in love; but perfect love casts out fear.
I John 4:18

FEAR-the thief of dreams, the destroyer of hopes.
FEAR-the paralyzer of visions, the undertaker of obedience.
FEAR: Face it. Hate it. Fight it. Overcome it.

𝕴t was a hot summer day in the inner city and I am standing in a park known as Jurassic Park. It became known as such because of the many acts of violence that occurred there. For most, it's a place to be avoided. There are no houses, no manicured lawns, nor flowers to admire. In fact, there's nothing that's pleasing to the natural eye, not here.

Homeless men, women, and children began to fill the park from all directions. As I watched different ones hurry to get in line for food, I wondered what had brought them to this place of homelessness. In spending time with various homeless people over the years, I'd heard a variety of stories and just as many explanations. Some were here because they chose to be and were perfectly happy to scrounge through garbage cans for food and other 'valuables'. Some were here because of the destructive spiral brought about by their various addictions. Others were here because of abuse that had devastated them, to the point that they were unable to cope with day-to-day life. And some were here because of tragic circumstances in life that were beyond their control.

I turned to one of my homeless friends and handed her a cold drink. Taking it, she smiled and said, *"Thanks, it sure is hot today."*

She took a long drink; sweat ran down her face and neck. Her hair was soaked and so was her shirt. She smelled as if she hadn't bathed in several weeks and probably hadn't. As she finished the last of the punch, I noticed her hands were trembling. I said, *"We brought turkey and cheese sandwiches tonight. Would you like one?"*

"Yeah, I sure would. I haven't eaten in a while."

As we walked arm in arm to the table, I noticed a homeless man sitting alone on the stone steps of the old church building across the street. A cat lay curled up on the step behind him. The man very slowly extended his hand toward the cat, offering it a piece of his hot dog. The cat's intense hunger overcame its obvious fear and the morsel was eagerly devoured. The man took a bite himself, then broke off another for the cat. He repeated this routine until the hot dog was finally consumed. At that point, the cat cautiously approached the man, curled up beside his feet and fell asleep.

This man's kindness touched me, so I quickly filled another plate and took it to him. As I approached, the cat darted around the corner.

"Hi, my name's Rhonda."

He hesitated and shifted somewhat nervously, then replied, *"My name's Anthony, but people call me Tony."*

"Would it be okay if I sat with you, Tony?"

Looking somewhat unsure, he answered, *"I guess it's okay."*

Handing him the plate of food, I said, *"I couldn't help but notice your kindness to that cat. I think the cat ate more of your hot dog than you did."*

Tony chuckled and noticeably relaxed. Taking a bite of his hot dog, he replied, *"Yeah, I kinda' felt sorry for the old, scruffy thing. It doesn't have a home, ya know."*

I pointed to the cat that had returned and was now hiding behind his leg and said, *"I think you just made a friend for life."*

"It's taken me a long time to get that cat to come near me cause it's really scared of people."

He paused, broke off another piece of hot dog and hand-fed the cat. *"I bet somebody's beat this cat and that's why it's so scared. Meanness does that to a person, ya know?"*

"Yeah, I know."

Tony shared another piece of his hot dog with his cat friend. Because of his comment, I suspected Tony had been abused. I whispered a quick prayer then said, *"Tony, I have a friend who was a lot like this cat. She was extremely afraid of people, but not anymore. Would you like to hear what changed her?"*

He laid down his empty plate, gently stroked the cat then answered, *"Sure."*

"My friend's name is Margaret, but everybody calls her Mocky. That's her over there by the grill. Anyway, when she first started coming here with us, she was so afraid of people that she wouldn't talk to anyone. But she loved coming and was determined not to let her fear stop her. She asked us to pray that God would help her, which we gladly did. The weeks came and went and Mocky continued coming. She worked really hard, but rarely talked.

Then, one icy night in January, everything changed for her. That night, Mocky and I were passing out cups of hot chocolate. After the steady stream of people were served, I leaned against the church wall trying to escape the bitter wind.

Across the street, several men sat huddled in front of a basement vent taking advantage of the tiny trickle of heat. As they ate the food we'd given them, a huge rat sat in the nearby shadows, waiting for a crumb to fall. It didn't have long to wait. A piece of bread fell and before the man could retrieve it, the rat raced out of the darkness, ran up the man's leg, snatched the bread from his lap, stuffed it in his mouth, then ran back to the shadows. With one gulp, the rather large piece of bread was gone. Surprisingly, none of the men reacted or even seemed to notice.

My whole body shivered at the sight of the rat on that man's belly. I looked away. The resident drug dealer was boldly promoting his goods on the opposite corner of the street. Mocky and I looked at each other and shook our heads. That was when we noticed him. Sitting alone on the top of these steps was a homeless man shivering violently. From the way he was stuffing the food in his mouth, I guessed he hadn't eaten in a while. He looked much older than most of the homeless men we had encountered. His face was very thin and quite wrinkled. His hair and beard were gray and matted. His stocking cap was more holes than hat. His gloves were paper-thin and missing several fingertips. He had on several shirts, obviously trying to keep out the cold.

Mocky couldn't take her eyes off him; her tender heart ached. The longer she watched, the more she wanted to go to him. But the familiar fear paralyzed her, causing her to turn away. She busied herself with straightening the clothes, but couldn't get his face out of her mind. Quickly she prayed, asking God for the courage to go to him. Taking a deep breath, she climbed the church steps with legs that were trembling, but not from the cold. Extending her hand, she said, "Hi, my name's Mocky. May I sit down?"

Obviously uneasy, he hesitated. Then he wiped his gloved hand on his pant leg, shook her extended hand and replied, "I'm Johnny."

Mocky sat down, not knowing what to say. There was nothing but silence for several long minutes. Johnny spoke first, "I was wondering—why do you bother coming down here in the cold and bringing food to no-goods like us?"

Without even thinking, Mocky answered, "Because Jesus loves you."

Johnny froze; his fork was halfway between his mouth and his plate. Mocky looked away, wondering what she should say next. Another long silence. Mustering all the courage she had, she looked back at him and tears were streaming down his face. His voice cracked as he said, "No one's ever said that to me, not ever."

Overcome with emotion, he was unable to say more.

Mocky was stunned at his response. A river of tears ran down her face as she told him Jesus loved him so much that He died for him. Johnny held his face in his hands, softly crying. Just then, another man sat down on the step directly below him. Hearing Johnny cry, the man turned around and stared. Johnny grabbed his plate and fled.

Mocky remained on the cold, stone steps allowing her tears to flow unhindered. Her words had been like an arrow that had pierced Johnny's heart allowing the love of God to flow into him. The words that Johnny had said washed over her. Her heart hurt for him and the many others who, like Johnny, had never heard those life-giving words. Her mind replayed Johnny's words. How could he have lived so long without hearing that Jesus loved him? How was that possible?

On the way home that night, Mocky told us about her experience. She said, 'I shudder to think that I almost allowed my fears to keep me from going to him. If I'd given in, like I usually do, then Johnny wouldn't have heard that Jesus loves him, and I would've missed one of the greatest moments of my life.'

Tony, I have to tell you, that experience changed Mocky. She was a different person from that night on. Her confidence grew and now she's one of the friendliest volunteers on our team."

I looked at Tony; his eyes were fixed on some unseen point. Finally, he asked, *"Do you suppose God would've sent someone else to tell Johnny He loved him, if Mocky had chickened out?"*

I answered, *"Maybe, maybe not. No one knows the answer to that question. What I do know is God doesn't ever want us to miss an opportunity to share His love with others. We can't allow fear to prevent us from sharing that good news. Tony, do you know that Jesus loves you?"*

"Yeah, I do. I'm a real believer. I know He died on the cross for me and I love Him for it. Jesus takes care of me and He's the only reason I'm still alive in this awful place. Not to change the subject, but I just gotta' know, did Mocky ever see Johnny again?"

"I'm so glad to hear that you're a believer. As for Johnny, Mocky diligently looked for him for months. But, sadly, she never saw him again. Who knows, perhaps one day, she'll see him in heaven."

"Boy, that's one reunion I'd like to see!" He exclaimed.
"So would I."

Tony smiled and said, *"I'm a lot like Mocky was. I'm really afraid of people; that's why I keep to myself. I don't like being this way; it makes for a lonely life. I'm glad you told me about Mocky. I'm going to do just what she did. When I'm afraid, which is often, I'm gonna pray and then I'm going to just do what I'm afraid of. Hey, thanks a lot."*

"Believe me, it's been my pleasure," I replied.

I got up to leave and Tony said, *"You were talkin' about the rat that ran up that guy's leg. The reason those guys didn't react was cause we get use to having rats hangin' around and even crawling on us, especially when we're asleep. It gets to where you don't think nuthin' about it after awhile. Why, I've seen rats down here as big as this here cat."*

A shiver ran up my spine—that's a big rat. I thought back to the first rat I saw here. I'd heard a noise behind me and turned around, expecting to see a dog or cat. Not more than two feet away were three really large rats aggressively licking the hot chocolate we had spilled just moments before. Of course, I did what any proper southern girl would do and flew up the steps to the highest point, screaming all the way. Several other ladies followed my example. Danny heard our screams and hurriedly pushed his way through the crowded sidewalk to slay our dragon. Seeing that it was 'just rats' he chuckled, but chased them away. He then took my hand and assured me it was safe to 'come down from the castle wall'.

Sitting back down beside Tony, I said, *"I'm really afraid of rats, any size—big or little. But even a rat as big as this cat wouldn't keep me from coming down here. I guess we all have fears that we must face because if we don't, those fears will prevent us from doing what's right. So, be encouraged and fight the good fight. Pray, and with God on your side, you'll win this battle."*

The following week, I watched while Tony stood in the food line. Then, instead of retreating to the steps, he sat down beside another homeless man. The weeks passed and he began to talk more and more to those around him. Several months later, for the first time in years, he applied for a job. He said, *"Even if I don't get the job, it's okay. The important thing is that I did it! I overcame my fear and filled out that application. And if I don't get this one, I'll just try someplace else. It's still not easy for me to talk to people, but it's not as bad as it used to be."*

Pulling a small New Testament out of his pocket and holding it up he said, *"I have a secret weapon."*

And what a mighty weapon it is!

* * * * * * * * * *

Tony didn't get that job, but did get hired as a cook in a small restaurant. About six months later, he visited us at Jurassic Park. He was doing really well and had saved enough money to rent a small apartment, where he lives with the cat he befriended on the stone steps.

Mocky freely loves on some inner city children.

A Song To Sing

But whoever has the world's goods,
And beholds his brother in need and closes his heart against him,
How does the love of God abide in him?
I John 3:17

Life is a song.
Sometimes the notes are sweet
And other times, they're bitter to the soul.
But through it all, there is One
Who knows every joy and feels every hurt.
And He has promised to see us through.

𝕴t was a very cold, winter night. My friends and I donned sweaters, gloves, hats and coats to make our weekly trip into the city. Armed with food, hot chocolate, coats and blankets, we offered kindness to homeless men, women and children.

As we passed out food, it seemed as if the very wind was fighting against us. We pulled our coats tightly around us. It wasn't long before we noticed a young girl sitting alone, leaning against a wall. A couple of us took her a steaming cup of cocoa and some hot food. She was very thin and quite pale. Her eyes were dull, as if the very color had faded from them. She wore a T-shirt, jeans, a thin jacket and tennis shoes. But, it wasn't what she was wearing

37

that struck me, but what she wasn't wearing. She had no socks, no gloves, and no coat. She coughed continuously and her body shivered from the bitter, icy wind.

Reaching out to take the plate I extended to her, she thanked us. We continued on to pass out the rest of the food. Yet, all the while, I kept looking back. There was something about this one, which compelled me to know more. What series of events had transpired in her life that had brought her to a place like this? I knew nothing about her; yet, my heart was drawn to her like a mother searching for a lost child. I knew I had to go back.

Returning, I sat beside her on the frozen sidewalk. She said her name was Gina. It wasn't long before another volunteer joined us; with a coat draped over her arm, which she gave to Gina. She took off her own gloves and gave them to this young girl. Laying aside her empty plate, Gina quickly slipped her frozen hands into the warm, thick gloves and snuggled into her new coat. Without any coaxing from us, Gina suddenly opened the pages of her heart and answered the question I'd asked myself earlier.

"I bet you wouldn't guess that I'm seventeen. When I was fifteen, my father had a heart attack and died—just like that. One day he was telling me how he loved the freckles on my nose and the next day he was gone. My stepmother went berserk and told me it was my fault he died. She said that if I'd been a better daughter he'd still be alive. I haven't been able to figure out what she thought I did that was so bad."

Pulling her legs up next to her body, she continued, *"A few weeks after my father's funeral, I came home from school and found all my things in boxes. My stepmother said I had to leave because her house wasn't big enough for both of us. I asked her where I should go and she said she didn't know and didn't care. Well, I didn't have anyplace to go, so for the past eighteen months, I've walked the streets, sleeping wherever I could, whenever I could. I'm not proud of it, but I've done things I never thought I'd do, just so I could eat. Out here on the streets, you do whatever it takes just to get through the day."*

No one moved, no one said anything. After all, what could we say in the face of such tragedy, such pain? We sat in the cold stillness, with only her coughs breaking the silence. She seemed to be looking far away, past the trash-strewn streets and the city lights, perhaps to a time when life was better, kinder. Shaking herself she looked in my tear-filled eyes. For a moment our hearts touched. With a quivering chin she asked, *"Do you think I really caused my father's heart attack?"*

Her eyes begged me to convince her it wasn't true. Her heart silently pleaded with me to deliver her from the chains holding her captive. I had just been given a glimpse of her world and saw how dark and hopeless it was. I understood that the depth of her painful song was far too deep for mere words to heal. But words were all I had—I assured her she wasn't responsible.

Then, we prayed, asking our heavenly Father to heal her and do what we were powerless to do. All too quickly, the time came for us to leave. How could we go home to our comfortable, warm houses and leave this girl here, sick and so cold, with no one to care for her? I searched for an answer. It seemed the only solution was to take her home with me. But how could I do that? After all, I didn't really know her. My mind quickly listed all the reasons why I shouldn't do this, but my heart screamed to embrace her. Several other volunteers expressed their concerns about leaving her. The tug-of-war going on inside of me grew to unbearable proportions. For me, there was no easy solution—except to do nothing.

Laying my hand on her shoulder I said, *"Gina, it's time for us to go. But, we'll be back next Thursday. We'll bring you some warm clothes and more food. Will you be okay?"*

As soon as I said it, I realized just how stupid that question was. Of course, she wouldn't be okay. She had no place to go. She'd sleep on the sidewalk and the temperature was already way below freezing. From the sound of her continuous cough, she was obviously sick.

Just then my daughter, Dana, asked, *"Gina, what size shoes do you wear?"*

"Six," she replied.

Without the slightest hesitation, Dana unlaced her size six shoes, handed them to Gina and joyfully said, *"Gina, these shoes are brand new. I just bought them yesterday and this is the first time they've ever been worn. I want you to have them."*

The safety latch on my heart came undone and the pent-up tears flooded my eyes. I knew what no one else there knew—Dana had worked diligently the past several months to earn the money to buy these particular shoes. Dana only had one pair of shoes at home and they were worn-out.

Gina quickly tried on her new shoes and for the first time that night, she smiled. Standing, she gave Dana a hug and exclaimed, *"They're perfect!"*

Gina threw her old shoes aside. I picked them up to toss in the nearby trash can. For some unknown reason, I turned them over. I couldn't believe my eyes. Gina had been wearing shoes that were nearly two sizes too small for her! I stood there trying to sort it all out. In the background, I heard Gina say, *"Just this morning I asked God for a pair of shoes because mine were too small and hurt my feet. I guess He heard me."*

I turned my attention back to the shoes still in my hands. I noticed how dirty the once white canvas was, how frazzled the once perfectly braided laces were, and how the heels were broken and crushed. The toes had holes in them and the soles were paper-thin in places. These shoes obviously had traveled many miles and walked down many hard roads. And yet, there was a time when these old, beat-up shoes were just as clean and attractive as the ones Gina now wore.

I realized I held in my hand a picture of Gina: crushed, broken, cast aside, unwanted, frazzled, tattered, and dirty. Her very existence was worn so thin that there wasn't much life left in her. Her smallness overwhelmed me. She was much too fragile to be alone in this harsh, ugly world. The weight of all she'd lost, all that was stolen from her, came into focus. So much pain crammed into such a tiny frame! The old shoes I held in my hands now took on a new look and I held them close.

I left that night thinking about two teenagers whose lives overlapped for just a moment in time. They both sang a song. One sang a song of pain and injustice. The other sang of joy and sacrificial giving. One left wearing only socks and went home to a warm bed, plenty of food and a loving family. The other, wearing new shoes, was found later that night unconscious on the sidewalk. An ambulance was called and Gina was rushed to the hospital where she was diagnosed with pneumonia.

We never saw Gina again.

* * * * * * * * * *

It's been over three years since that night and I still think of Gina. I wonder where she is and what she's doing. I wonder what song she now sings?

As for Dana, the following day, someone heard that she'd given away her shoes so they gave her some money to buy another pair of shoes. Since that day, Dana has experienced God's supernatural provision numerous times regarding shoes. For example, when those shoes wore out, she prayed for a particular shoe and the very next day someone from church gave us several boxes of clothing. As Dana and I sorted the clothing, she found the identical pair she'd asked the Lord for. They were brand new and just happened to be her size! Another example happened just two days ago when Dana was shopping with her sister. Dana was looking for a particular style of black boots. She found the exact pair and they were on sale for $2.00.

God clearly sees all.

Burl happy to have a guitar again.

CHAPTER FIVE

No Where To Go

My sheep hear My voice, and I know them, and they follow Me;
And I give eternal life to them, and they shall never perish;
And no one shall snatch them out of My hand.
John 10:27,28

Everyone is a masterpiece...waiting to be discovered.
Everyone is a masterpiece...
in different stages of completion.
Everyone is a masterpiece...
lovingly formed by the Master's hand.

𝕿here were about thirty people standing in the food line today at Jurassic Park. It was good to see the friends we had made. I saw Debbie, Tyrone, and Larry, but where was Burl? I hadn't seen him since before his surgery three weeks earlier. I was very concerned and continued scanning the park.

I saw our resident chef, Richard, grilling hot dogs to perfection and thought back to the first time he came downtown with us. Several of our volunteers were out of town, so Danny asked Richard if he'd help out. He agreed, but said he'd only come if he didn't have to talk to anyone. That was no problem.

That first night, Richard grilled a multitude of hot dogs without saying one word. On the way home, Richard asked if we needed his help the next week. And so it was week after week, Richard came and quietly served, each time asking if we needed his help for the next week. As the months passed, Richard began talking to us and to the homeless. Now, more than two years later, Richard not only talks freely and comfortably to anyone who will listen, but often has us in stitches with his jokes. He's a real delight.

The wind shifted and blew smoke from the grill in my face, so I shut my eyes. For a moment, I was in my backyard among the flowers, trees and singing birds enjoying a barbecue. But just as quickly, a speeding car squealed down the street jerking me back to reality and the harsh, ever-present dangers of the inner city.

Resuming my search for Burl, I saw another faithful volunteer, Jenny. She was down on her knees sorting through a mountain of clothing. On her back was her six-month-old and by her side was her three-year-old daughter. She was helping an elderly lady look for clothing. Suddenly, Jenny held up a bright, yellow dress and said, *"This looks like it will fit you perfectly."*

The lady held it up against her body and replied, *"I believe it will. It's pretty, too."*

She quickly placed it in her plastic bag; then she and Jenny continued their search.

There, behind Jenny, was Barbara. She was intensely listening as an elderly homeless man poured out his troubles. She laid her hand on his shoulder, her way of saying; 'I care about you.' Soon, they both bowed their heads. Tears flowed down both their faces and my heart overflowed—how beautiful!

At the tables, Rod handed a young boy a plate with two hot dog buns. Dana asked if he'd like some chips and a muffin. Jamell, a teen who was part of Youth Explosion (our ministry to inner city teens) handed him a cup of what we all called, 'Danny's Special Punch'. Among the homeless, Danny's quite famous for his punch concoction. No one has figured out exactly what it is and I suspect never will. As far as the homeless are concerned, it's the best stuff around and that's saying a lot, if you know what I mean.

To my great relief, I finally saw Burl coming around the corner of a nearby building. He was walking slowly, his head was down and his hands were in his pockets. Without stopping to talk with anyone, which was unusual, he walked directly to the hot dog line. I watched his kindness prevail over his obvious despondency, as he offered the lady standing in line behind him to go first.

I hurried over to Burl and laid my hand on his sagging shoulder. He looked up and attempted a smile. This was definitely not the happy, upbeat Burl I'd known for several years.

"How are you, Burl?"

He replied, *"Physically I'm feeling much better, but this has been a very hard week for me."*

"What happened?"

Burl had reached the front of the line and Rod greeted him warmly. He handed him a plate, then said, *"It's so good to see you, Burl. How'd your surgery go?"*

"It went well, thanks. My doctor said it looks like they got all the cancer."

Burl was one of our favorites among the homeless. I grabbed a blueberry muffin and followed Burl to the tarp we'd spread on the ground. Carefully balancing his full plate, he sat down. I sat beside him. He bowed his head and prayed. Raising his head, he looked out across the park. There was much sadness in his voice as he said, *"I never would've thought in a million years I'd be living in a homeless shelter. I've been here almost five years now and it's still hard for me to believe. Some days it's much harder than others."*

I took a deep breath and said, *"Burl, I can't imagine what it must be like for you and neither can so many others out there. I'd love to have an opportunity to tell your story to others. I was wondering if you'd give me permission to tell your story in this book I'm writing."*

Obviously surprised, he asked, *"Why in the world would you want to write about me?"*

"Burl, people need to hear your story. They need to know that all homeless people are not homeless because of drugs or alcohol or laziness. They need to know that sometimes circumstances happen to a person that are unavoidable. Your story's the perfect example of that. What do you think?"

With my recorder and notebook in hand, I waited. After a long moment, Burl answered, *"Well, where should I start?"*

"At the beginning would be good."

Setting his plate aside he began, *"I was born in Lee's Summit, Missouri in 1936. My mother was a Christian but my father refused to have anything to do with religion. When I was thirteen, a nearby church offered to pick my four brothers and me up for Sunday school. For the first time in my life, I attended church. I listened as the Sunday school teacher talked about Jesus, but I was having trouble understanding it all. As the weeks passed, I grew intrigued by the other teens and their intense interest in the bible. They talked about Jesus like they knew Him or something. The more I was around them, the more curious I became. They didn't cuss, smoke or drink and they seemed so happy. Because I was so miserable, I wanted what they had and yet, I couldn't figure out exactly what that was.*

One day after church, I asked the pastor why everyone seemed so happy. To my surprise, he stopped what he was doing and sat down beside me. He said he knew exactly what it was that made them happy. That was when he told me all about Jesus and how we're all sinners, including me. He said we all deserve to be punished for our sins, but Jesus had taken our place and died so that we might live. He said that when we accept Jesus as our Lord and Savior, we're forgiven of all our sins and Jesus fills us with His joy. By the time he was finished, I was squirming in my seat. I could hardly wait to ask Jesus to forgive me. I prayed with the pastor and joy filled me just like he said. In that one moment, my whole life was changed.

The years passed and I became an electrician, got married and had two beautiful children. Everything was going very well for me. I was living the American dream. That is, until October of 1993, when without any warning I had a heart attack. The following day, I had open-heart surgery. Just two days later, my wife walked into my hospital room and announced she was leaving me. She walked out of my hospital room and out of my life, offering no explanation or apologies. Three days later, I went home to an empty house.

Then, in January of 1994, I got very sick and was admitted to the hospital again. This time I had gallbladder surgery. It had been almost four months since I'd been able to work and as a result, I was financially ruined.

The day I was dismissed from the hospital, I didn't have a penny to my name. I'd lost my car, my home, everything. I had no where to go. The Veteran's Administration found me a room in a homeless shelter and was kind enough to drive me here.

I was now living in an environment that was very strange and completely foreign to me. The constant use of drugs and alcohol by many of the people around me threatened to make me a hermit. The poverty I experienced was depressing and I struggled to find contentment in the midst of nothing. Not only was I penniless, but I was alone and in some ways, that was much harder than the poverty.

As soon as I was well enough, I found a job driving an ice cream truck. It felt good to be doing something productive again. Soon after, I heard about a church on Independence Avenue, so I visited there. Immediately, I felt at home and quickly became active in the life of that church. One night, after work, I came home to the shelter and noticed a group of people cooking hot dogs in the park. Curiosity got the best of me, so I went over to see what was going on. That's when I met all of you. Everyone was very friendly and I really enjoyed your company. You really encouraged me.

Then, a couple of months ago, I got sick again and had to quit driving my ice cream truck. That's when the doctors found the cancer."

Burl stopped talking, and I asked, *"Burl, would you move out of the homeless shelter if you could?"*

Without hesitating, he replied, *"Yeah, I'd be out of here in a heartbeat. As a matter of fact, I plan to move as soon as I start drawing my social security check. I won't move far though because I want to stay close to my church. I don't mind living in the inner city. Most of the time, it's not too bad. I keep to myself. As long as you don't drink or use drugs, you won't have too much trouble, except for all the stealing that goes on. The only thing I had left when I moved here was my guitar. I just loved strumming and singing that old thing, but it wasn't long before someone broke in my room and stole it while I was at work. That was very hard for me to take. But, mostly, I don't have much trouble. Just the other day someone asked me for money, so he could buy liquor. I asked him why he thought I'd give him money for liquor, when I don't drink the stuff myself. He quickly moved on to the next guy because he knew I had a point. In a place like this, it's important to stand up for what's right and not give into the pressures that are all around you. But, I guess that's true no matter where you live."*

"Burl, you're such a strong, Godly man. How is it that you've gone through so many difficult things without growing bitter or turning your back on God?"

He smiled, shook his head, then replied, *"Don't misunderstand, I'm human just like the next guy. I'm not some super hero. Believe me, I've had moments when I was tempted to quit on God and everything else. I've certainly made more than my share of mistakes through the years, but I've learned to take them to God. He's faithful to forgive and help me. I do my best to obey God's word and stay connected to my church family; there's much wisdom in that.*

Just this week, I'm teaching at vacation bible school. I take the guitar your friend Jim gave me and play it for the kids. It makes them happy and that makes me happy. It troubles me when I see sadness in a child's eyes. Today, a little fella kept calling me daddy. After quite some time, I asked him where his daddy was. He said he didn't have one. I asked him if he had a grandpa, he said no then asked if I'd be his grandpa. Of course I said yes. That little fella grinned from ear to ear and squeezed my leg like there was no tomorrow. Things like that keep me from feeling sorry for myself. It really breaks my heart to see the conditions a lot of these children live in. It causes me to realize I don't really have it so bad. I do the best I can each day and trust God to see me through. That's all I can do, that's all anyone can do."

I asked, *"Burl, I know this question might be difficult to answer. But, I was wondering, what's been the hardest thing you've gone through?"*

He answered, *"Without a doubt, the cancer. It's changed the way I look at everything. I sure appreciate life a lot more now. People live like they have all the time in the world; I use to think that way too, but not anymore. This cancer has opened my eyes to how uncertain life is. There are no guarantees. We could be gone just like that."* He snapped his fingers and continued, *"If I hadn't known the Lord, I wouldn't have made it in this old world. It's a tough place, there's only one way to live and that's to know Jesus personally and follow Him the best you can. That's what I try to do everyday. I haven't arrived, yet. But, I've discovered that Jesus knows how to take care of us really well."*

The man beside me was living proof of that.

The sun was sinking behind the tall buildings, casting its golden light all around us. I looked back at Burl. The glorious light from the sun covered his face. How appropriate—this man truly was a light in the midst of a dark world. Sin, filth, poverty, loneliness, disappointment and hopelessness surrounded him, yet he kept his eyes fixed on his eternal destination—heaven. Burl had become a beautiful masterpiece in the hands of his Maker.

Burl is a man without a home of his own, but in heaven's eyes that's only temporary. He has a home waiting for him somewhere beyond that golden, setting sun.

* * * * * * * * *

Over two years have passed since Burl had his cancer surgery. To this day he remains cancer-free. He has moved out of the home-less shelter and now lives in a small apartment near his church family.

CHAPTER SIX

Dancing in the Rain

And coming to Him as a living stone, rejected by men,
But choice and precious in the sight of God.
I Peter 2:4

April showers bring May flowers—every time!

𝕴n the first two-and-a-half years of feeding the homeless, it had never rained on us and I was much too proud of that fact.

It had happened slowly, but still, it had happened. I'd come to the point where I believed our ministry was God's gift to the homeless. Obviously, God must've been in agreement, thus the withholding of rain. After all, two years, seven months and two weeks of no rain on Thursday nights had to be a record.

Somewhere, along the way, I'd forgotten the fact that anything and everything I do is only by the grace of God. I had absolutely nothing to be proud of. I knew the Lord loved me because of who He is and not because of anything I do. Yet, pride was rearing its ugly head in my life and I was completely unaware of it. Thankfully, we have a Savior who loves us so much, that He exposes the things in our hearts that fall short of His character. And so it was that God set the stage for me to come face to face with my arrogance and self-centeredness.

One Thursday evening, as we were on our way downtown, the sky suddenly grew black. Within minutes rain fell in torrents around us and the road was quickly covered with two or three inches of water. Water ran into the storm drains like a river rushing downstream. Behind us the sky was clear, but ahead of us the sky was black with heavy rain clouds. Disappointment flooded me, as I thought about my perfect record being swept away with this incredible downpour.

We began to pray, asking the Lord to stop the rain. I said the right words, but my motives were clearly less than pure. Looking out the van window, there was no hope in sight. We talked of turning around, but because we were so close to Jurassic Park, we decided to keep going. Perhaps, God would stop the rain for us.

To our amazement, that's exactly what happened. We were just a few blocks from the park when the rain abruptly and instantly stopped! The clouds parted like the Red Sea before Moses and the sunlight broke through the darkness, filling us with joy! You can imagine how I felt—now I was even more convinced that we were God's gift to the homeless.

The sun continued to burn away the clouds as we pulled into our usual parking place. Because of the rain, the usual crowd wasn't waiting for us. Tim, one of our long-time homeless friends leaned against a sign on the corner. He wore the same T-shirt, faded cut-off jeans, and old tennis shoes that he wore each week. Over his shoulder hung a soggy backpack that held his few earthly belongings. He was drenched. Nevertheless, he had a big smile on his face, exposing his missing front teeth.

Our eyes met and he waved wildly. This was quite unusual, as he's normally mild-mannered and quite reserved. He made his way across the street shouting, *"Hey, I've got something to tell you! You're not going to believe it!"*

Tim's eyes were alive and his voice was electric. I'd never seen him like this. I couldn't help but smile. Slinging his backpack on the ground, he blurted out, *"I was on my way to the park when it started raining. No problem, I thought, I don't mind the rain so much. It was a nice break from this awful, hot weather we've had this past week. Anyway, I walked a few steps, then I thought about you guys and how you were going to get soaked.*

Well, I kept walking and thinking. I thought about how you come each week and feed us. The more I thought about you guys, the more disturbed I got. Finally, out of desperation, I decided to pray. I ain't ever prayed before, so I wasn't sure how. I just said, 'God, if you're really who these people say you are, then I'd be much obliged if you'd stop this rain. It doesn't seem right for these folks to come down here and get wet. And if it keeps on raining, they won't be able to feed anybody anyway. I'm really hoping you'll see fit to stop this here rain before it's too late. Amen.'

I stood there waiting. Nothing happened, the rain was falling just as hard as ever. I shrugged and said, 'Oh, well, I reckon I was right, there ain't nobody up there.' I took about five steps, when the rain suddenly stopped! Just like that. I couldn't believe it. I froze in my tracks; I think I even stopped breathing. I looked up real slow and it was like a light came on and I knew God was real and He'd heard me. I laughed and jumped and shouted, 'By golly, God's real! Not only is He real but He heard me talkin' to Him!'

I started dancing around and it felt like heavy weights were being lifted off my shoulders. For the first time in my life, I felt free. I danced. I laughed. I clapped. All the way down here, I partied. I could hardly wait for you guys to get here. You really were right about God and now I know it."

I stood in silence before this man who, by most people's standards, would generally be viewed as worthless. This is a man without a job or paycheck. He doesn't have a car, or a house, or a bank account. He's extremely skinny, wears rags for clothes, his hair is almost always dirty and he's missing several teeth.

I was thrilled God had made His presence known to Tim. My soul was warmed in a deep way for him. Yet, at the same time, I felt deep conviction in my own heart. I was shocked by the truth that Tim's story revealed. I hadn't once thought of him, only my perfect record.

I looked closely at Tim, trying to brand this moment forever on my heart. There he stood with his wet hair, soaked clothes and happy face. This was one lesson I didn't want to ever forget.

While we handed out food and clothing, Tim went from person to person telling anyone who'd listen about his encounter with

God. The sun was setting, sending its orange rays our way. It felt like a warm smile. I thought of the Savior Who, I was certain was smiling too.

The time passed quickly and we said good-bye to Tim. Just as Danny started the van, the heavens opened and rain came pouring down! Not believing my eyes, I turned to see Tim's reaction. It wasn't hard to find him amongst the crowd—he was easy to recognize, even in the dark—he was the only one dancing in the rain.

* * * * * * * * * *

Later that night, confessing my selfish behavior and arrogance to the Lord, I heard a quiet voice speak to my heart, *"You remember you're only human and I'll remember I've washed you in My blood making you clean."*

How thankful I am for His blood that washes away my sins!

Two people were going to the same place from different directions. Both were confronted by the same circumstances, but each responded differently. I saw the rain and thought of myself. Tim saw the rain and thought of us. He experienced a God, Who changed his life. And his experience brought me face to face with myself and changed me, too. Am I ever grateful for the rain!

Two years have passed since Tim's life-changing encounter with God. During that time, Tim faithfully worked alongside us, helping unload the van and passing out food and clothing.

Just recently, Tim said, *"Well, I've good news and bad news. I finally found a job. That's the good news. The bad news is that I won't be able to help anymore because I'll be working the night shift."*

We were happy he'd found a job, but very sad that we wouldn't see him again. And we told him so. He lowered his head, kicked at a rock with the toe of his shoe and said, *"Yeah, I'm going to miss you guys a whole lot, too."*

We prayed together for the last time that night, then said good-bye. I watched Tim walk down the sidewalk with his backpack on his shoulder. I looked up to the heavens. The sun was setting and painted the sky a deep reddish-orange.

There were no clouds in the sky or rain in sight.

CHAPTER SEVEN

The Angel With Skinny Legs

Do not neglect to show hospitality to strangers
For by this some have entertained angels without knowing it.
Hebrews 13:2

Angels move among us unnoticed,
Bringing declarations of the Father's love.
Angels dressed in common attire
Speaking uncommon words from Father above.

Early one morning, as I was praying, from out of nowhere this phrase interrupted my thoughts, *"Tonight, you will meet an angel."*

Was that God? I sat quietly, waiting and wondering. After receiving no further revelation, I closed my bible and went about my daily activities. Later that evening, while preparing dinner, once again that still, small voice interrupted my thoughts with this phrase: *'Angels among us.'*

Just then, my daughter, Misty, walked into the kitchen and I told her about my 'messages'.

She responded, *"Mom, 'Angels Among Us' is the name of a song."*

Just then, my husband Danny phoned and said, *"I'm going to be late because I'm stuck in traffic. By the way, I just heard a song on the radio I think you'd like."*

Only vaguely interested, I asked, *"What's the name of it?"*
"It's called, 'Angels Among Us.'"
Now he had my full attention. Putting my spoon down I asked,
"What did you say?"
He replied, *"It's called, 'Angels Among Us.' I thought of you
when I heard it. I think you'd like it."*
*"That's what I thought you said. Let me tell you what hap-
pened today..."*
After hearing about my two previous 'experiences', he re-
sponded, *"Well, tonight should be quite interesting."*
We hung up and my imagination ran wild. What would it be
like to see an angel? What would it look like? I pictured an angel
with a beautiful face, golden hair, large wings and dazzling white
attire. This was definitely going to be exciting.
The homeless team arrived to help prepare the food. My excitement only increased as I told them about my angel messages.
Having filled approximately 150 plates, we loaded the van. In
doing so, I showed everyone a brand new leopard blanket that had
been donated. I suggested we save it for someone special, someone who wouldn't trade it for drugs or alcohol. Everyone agreed,
so I placed it under the seat.
We arrived at our usual location where a group of the homeless
were huddled together, trying desperately to protect themselves from
the icy wind. I soon forgot about the possibility of meeting an
angel because of the furious activity that's involved in setting up
our food, clothing and blanket distribution.
About halfway through our time there, Mary Lee pointed out a
small group standing at the other end of the block. We walked
over and invited them to join us for dinner. Just as we turned to
head back, we noticed a little woman scampering across the street
like a happy, little squirrel searching for acorns. Her child-likeness
was so foreign to this oppressive place, that we stopped to watch
her.
She was very small and fragile-looking. Her jean jacket was a
bit too small and barely reached her tiny waist. Her orange and
green skirt just covered her knees. I was fascinated by how skinny
her legs were. Bright green, open-toed shoes were all that covered

her feet; where were her socks? She wore no gloves, no hat and no coat. Her clothing was definitely less than adequate for the freezing temperatures.

She came to an abrupt halt within a few feet of us. Her bright, happy eyes brought a smile to my face. We introduced ourselves, then said, *"We have some hot food and warm clothes at that van over there. You're welcome to join us."*

She replied, *"No thank you for the food and clothing. All I really need is a blanket."*

Mary Lee, not remembering the leopard blanket, said, *"I'm so sorry but we've already given away all the blankets. If you come back next week we'll have more."*

Mary Lee's response didn't seem to faze her. She sweetly smiled. I was so fascinated by the fact that her teeth were not chattering and her body wasn't trembling that I only vaguely heard their conversation. Mary Lee touched my arm, bringing me back to reality and said, *"Next week we need to save a blanket for this lady."*

I thought of the leopard blanket under the seat. Instantly, a tug of war began inside of me—to give or not to give? I didn't have anyone else in mind to give the blanket to, but I had hoped to give it to someone we knew. I looked closer at her, trying to decide if she was 'worthy'. I'd almost decided to keep silent about the blanket, when she stepped right in front of me, looked directly into my eyes, and said, *"I really do need a blanket. I know I don't look very special, but I promise not to trade it for drugs or alcohol."*

At this point, you could've knocked me over with a feather—she'd used the exact words I used earlier when describing the person we should give the blanket to! That was good enough for me. I asked her to wait and ran to retrieve the blanket from its hiding place. Returning, out of breath, I handed it to her and said, *"We were saving this blanket for someone special and that someone is you!"*

Immediately, she grabbed me and held me tightly. Then, she whispered in my ear, *"God blesses you for what you're doing here. He thanks you for loving His children and He wants you to know that He loves you deeply."*

With her words came an indescribable warmth that flowed throughout my entire body! I couldn't move; my feet felt as if they were glued to the sidewalk. I looked at her face and once again she looked directly into my tear-filled eyes and smiled. All I could do was nod in response. Tucking the leopard blanket under her arm, she skipped a short distance away then turned and waved good-bye.

For some reason, at that moment, I remembered the angel messages. She didn't look at all like an angel; at least not what I thought an angel should look like. Looking at Mary Lee, I whispered, *"The angel?"*

Without another word, Mary Lee and I ran to the corner. We looked up and down the street. There were several homeless men leaning against the buildings, but no women and no leopard blanket. Where could she have gone? It would've been impossible for her to get to the other end of the street that fast. There were no doors for her to slip into, no cars, nowhere to hide. There was absolutely no explanation for her disappearance.

No explanation, except maybe, just maybe, she was an angel. An angel who looked nothing like what I expected, but who brought a wonderful and very encouraging message to me.

* * * * * * * * * *

I never saw her again.

I possibly came close to missing out on a blessing that night. All because of the standard I used to determine who was 'special' and who wasn't. My standard was based on outward appearance. That was terribly wrong.

I've often thought of those wonderful words spoken to me that day and wondered if I hadn't given her that blanket, would she still have delivered her message? I don't know. But, I'm so thankful God doesn't leave us in our flawed state, but pursues us and changes us.

I learned a valuable lesson that night. I learned just how important it is not to judge a book by its cover—because there just might be an angel hiding behind it.

CHAPTER EIGHT

Love Never Fails

Love is patient, love is kind, and is not jealous;
Love doesn't brag and is not arrogant.
Love bears all things, believes all things,
Hopes all things, endures all things.
Love never fails...
I Cor. 13: 4,7-8

Nothing you do unto Him is ever wasted.

One evening, Kenny came home from work and found his four young children alone. Stephen, his eight-year-old son, met him at the front door and said, *"Mom said to tell you she's gone to Ohio with her boyfriend and won't be back."*

Kenny hurried into the bedroom and found numerous clothes hangers scattered on the unmade bed. The dresser drawers were open and very empty. Her jewelry box was gone and so was the make-up that usually cluttered the top of her dresser.

Kenny's nine-year-old daughter, Jenny, leaned against him and said, *"Daddy, she took all her things, but she didn't take us."*

Tears cascaded down her beautiful, little face.

Kenny looked around his small house in disbelief. His four children, ages nine, eight, six and three, stood in the doorway waiting for dad to make everything right. Kenny sat down on the edge of the bed and whispered, *"What am I going to do?"*

Stephen walked over, laid his hand on his dad's drooping shoulders and answered, *"Don't worry, dad. I'll help you. We'll be just fine, you'll see."*

Unable to pay the bills without his wife's paycheck, Kenny and his children had no other option but to move in with his parents. Just six weeks later, Kenny's mother told him they were going to have to leave because four children in her house were just too many. The next day, she drove them to a homeless shelter and left them there.

That Thursday night, when we arrived at Jurassic Park, there were four beautiful children sitting on the church steps. It was obvious they were very sad. As soon as the van came to a stop, the doors flew open and several of us moms hurried to their side. Immediately, young Stephen said, *"We don't have a mom cause she ran off with her boyfriend. Now we're living in the homeless shelter because my grandma doesn't want us, either."*

Instantly, our hearts were captured and we went into action searching through the boxes for warm clothing, while plates were being filled with spaghetti. The three-year-old was wearing shorts and the night air was quite cool, so a blanket was quickly wrapped around her, as she snuggled on Mocky's lap.

Danny noticed Kenny standing in the background watching what was going on with his children. Grabbing a large plate of spaghetti, he went to him and said, *"Hi, I'm Danny."*

"I'm Kenny. Those are my kids."

"They sure look like great kids. I've got two of my own, who're really special."

Kenny took the plate of food and said, *"Things in my life are crazy right now. I don't think it could get any worse. My wife left me for another man. I lost my home and my job. My mother threw us out. So, I guess you could say things are as bad as they could get."*

"I'm really sorry. You must be in a world of hurt. I know someone who can help you. He has all the answers to all your problems. His name is Jesus. Do you know Him?"

Kenny answered, *"Not really. I never really thought much about Jesus, probably because I haven't really needed Him. But, I sure need some help now."*

"You know, Kenny, we all need Jesus in our lives. Sometimes, it just takes a while to realize it."

Danny talked with him in depth about Jesus and later that night, under a dim streetlight, surrounded by drinking, smoking, cursing and drug activity, Danny listened as Kenny accepted Jesus as his savior. Both men were crying.

Danny gave Kenny a bible and encouraged him to read the book of John. Kenny tried to give it back, but Danny insisted he keep it. I gave Stephen a children's bible and asked him to read it to his brother and sisters. The following week, an excited Stephen and Jenny told me about the bible stories they'd read. When asked if their dad had read any of the stories to them, Stephen replied, *"My dad can't read so he asked me to read to him."* Looking quite pleased, he continued, *"So, I read my bible to my whole family every night!"*

Just before we left, Kenny asked, *"Could me and the kids go to church with you on Sunday?"*

That was the beginning. The beginning of completely falling in love with his children. Each Sunday, Kenny and his children rode to church with us. I learned about life in a homeless shelter from a nine-year-old girl and an eight-year-old boy. I heard about the rats, the roaches, the filthy language, the violence, the sexual advances made toward innocent children, and other things too obscene to talk about. Week after week, I listened and my heart cried. This was no place for anyone, much less children.

It wasn't long after this that our ministry was presented with an opportunity to lease a house in the city. After much prayer, we signed the lease with the goal of housing homeless single parents and their children. With the help of many, we cleaned, painted and collected household furniture and supplies. Two very wonderful people volunteered to be house-parents. We were now ready; Kenny and his children were the first to move in.

All the painting was finished except the hallway, so I recruited Jenny to help me. As we rolled on the white paint, I said, *"Jenny, see these dirty walls, that's the way our hearts look before we know Jesus. Sin does that to us. Sin makes us all dirty and nasty on the inside, just like this wall. But when we ask Jesus to be our Lord and Savior, His blood covers us just like this white paint. His blood washes our sins away, making us white as snow, just like that wall we just painted."*

I looked at Jenny; she'd laid down her paintbrush. Her cute, little nose had paint sprinkles all over it. Her shoulder-length, brown hair was also splattered with paint. I asked if she'd like to give her life to Jesus.

She looked at me with her crystal-blue eyes and abruptly burst into tears. She nearly shouted, *"No! I can't to do that!"*

"Sure you can, I'll help you."

She replied, *"No, I can't because I don't want to lose my mind and go crazy. My mom and grandmother said that Christians are crazy and they've all lost their minds."*

I would've laughed except for her obvious distress. We talked for a while then I asked, *"Do you think I'm crazy?"*

She was silent for a moment then answered, *"I don't think so. But I think I should watch you just to make sure."*

"That sounds fair to me." I responded and silently prayed for the Lord to capture her heart.

Some weeks later, Valerie, one of the Sunday school teachers said to me, *"Keith has been in my Sunday school class for several months and I've never seen him smile and he almost never talks. He's always very withdrawn and quiet in my class. I've never seen a child so emotionless."* (Keith was hit in the head with a hammer by a relative when he was a two-year-old. He suffers seizures and has a severe learning disability because of it. But his heart is as tender and loving as any child I've ever known.) Valerie went on to say, *"Today I passed around the missionary can so the children could put their money in it. When the can was passed to Keith his face instantly came alive! His dull eyes grew bright and a big smile appeared on his face! He pointed to the photograph taped on the can and exclaimed, 'Danny and Rhonda! I love Danny and Rhonda!'"*

That day, I was overwhelmed by the love of a precious little boy. I thought of the scripture, "Love never fails." (I Corinthians 13:8). In this case, love had broken through and touched the heart of a little boy that nothing else had been able to penetrate. During the weeks that followed, Jenny continued to remind me that she was watching for any signs that I might be crazy. She was so eager to hear about Jesus that, often, she'd snuggle beside me and ask, *"Will you tell me another Jesus story?"*

Then, one day after one of those stories, she said, *"You sure don't act like you're crazy."* Then ran outside to play. Less than a week later, the day finally came we'd been praying for. The children and I were playing cards, when Jenny suddenly threw down her cards and said, *"I'll do it! I've decided I want to ask Jesus into my heart. I'll do it, even if I go crazy."*

Stephen looked up and simply said, *"Me too."*

What a glorious moment! There is nothing in this life as exciting as someone giving their lives to Jesus. It just doesn't get any better than that.

A couple of months later, it was Stephen's ninth birthday. We ate cake and ice cream until we were stuffed. Kenny could hardly wait to give Stephen the bicycle he'd bought for him. It was Stephen's first bicycle. Stephen was speechless and unable to move for a few minutes, then he exploded with squeals and much jumping.

Every day, he rode his bike up and down the sidewalk, careful to stay within the prescribed boundaries. I was impressed with his eagerness to share his bike with Jenny. Oftentimes, he'd get off the bike and offer it to her while he stood and watched. Other times, they'd ride double laughing as they struggled to keep the bike balanced. What fun they had!

Stephen was very careful with his bike, making sure it was locked in the basement when he wasn't riding it. Then, approximately four weeks after his birthday, Stephen called and through stifled tears said, *"Somebody's stolen my bike."*

"What? How'd they steal it? Did you leave it outside?"

"No. I locked it in the basement just like I always do. This morning, before I left for school, I checked on it just like always and it was there. But when I got home it was gone."

There was no explanation for the bicycle's disappearance. Stephen was heart-broken. Over the next couple of weeks, other things disappeared from the house. We suspected Kenny was selling these things, so we asked the Lord to expose him if he was guilty. Several days later, Kenny was caught passing a small table out the window to the neighborhood drug dealer.

As we talked with him, he confessed he was using a street drug called 'crack'. With his confession came a sickening thought. I had to know, *"Kenny, did you sell your son's bike?"*

With head down he answered, *"Yeah."*

Unable to bear what I heard, I ran upstairs to be with his children. We sat on the floor and I held little Emily and Keith on my lap. Jenny and Stephen each hung onto one of my arms. We talked about what had happened, then sang 'Jesus Loves Me' and 'Jesus Loves the Little Children' over and over. Finally, Jenny asked, *"Daddy said we're going to leave, is it true?"*

I answered, *"Sweetie, I don't know, but I want you to promise me something. Promise that no matter what happens in your life, you'll always remember that Jesus loves you and He's always there for you. Remember, no matter where you are or what's happening, He's right there with you."*

They promised. I read them a bible story, tucked them in bed and kissed their sweet, little faces. Shutting the door behind me, I leaned against it and wept the bitter tears I'd been fighting to hold back.

Late that night, Kenny woke his children, dressed them and slipped silently out the backdoor in pursuit of a cruel, white powder called crack.

* * * * * * * * * *

I grieved over this family for a long time. What more could we have done or said? Finally, the long awaited day came when I found peace. I thought of little Keith and the power of love in his life and realized we'd done all we could, we had loved them. I have it on good authority that love *never* fails.

It's been almost three years since that day. Recently, Danny and I saw Kenny at Jurassic Park buying some drugs. In talking with him, we found out his children had gone to live with his ex-wife. Kenny looked much older than his thirty-two years. The drugs were consuming his life. After a short visit, Kenny said good-bye, walked a short distance away, stopped, turned around and said, *"I'm really sorry."*

Then he walked on.

CHAPTER NINE

All of a Sudden

And let us not lose heart in doing good,
For in due time we shall reap if we do not grow weary.
Galatians 6:9

We go through life planting seeds,
never knowing if they'll live or die.
Then, one day, we look through the window of our life
And see our garden in full bloom.

𝕴t was Thursday night and as usual we were in our favorite place, Jurassic Park. Danny went about his regular 'job' of over-seeing the homeless team, but without his normal cheerful singing and whistling. He'd had a difficult week and was in great need of encouragement. He was picking up empty plates, when a man walked up behind him and said, *"I bet you don't remember me."*

Danny, turned, shook the man's outstretched hand and said, *"Of course, I remember you. How are you, James?"*

"Hey, I'm impressed. I'm doing just great. I've been trying to get here for several weeks and this week I told myself I was coming, no matter what. I wanted to let you know what's been going on in my life since the last time I saw you."

The two men sat down on the stone steps, James continued, *"When I first met you guys, I was sleeping on the streets, and in so much pain, I'd decided life wasn't worth the effort. Man, I was beyond lonely. You gave me food and clothes and that was good, but what I didn't expect was your friendship. You made me feel like I was somebody. Well, one night you told me that I'd never be happy unless I got right with God. I didn't believe you, but I began to notice how you were always humming, whistling or singing. I'd never met anybody who was that happy. Each week, you encouraged me to change and I began to believe I could do something with my life besides waste it. Then, one night, as I sat in the park feeling miserable, I watched a group of guys shouting obscenities at each other, doing their best to start a fight. Several girls joined in the ruckus and added fuel to the fire. I was disgusted and looked away. Just a few feet from me were several rats devouring some discarded food. I was so hungry, I found myself looking for something to fight off the rats with. Then, all of a sudden, everything got crystal clear and I was thoroughly disgusted with my life. I know this sounds weird but in that instant, I felt an overwhelming need for God. I fell down on my knees right there in front of everybody and prayed. I got up from there a changed man. I walked to the mission and got a bed for the night. The next morning, I took a shower and they gave me some clean clothes. It wasn't long before I found a job. Since then, I've worked really hard and saved my money. I now have an apartment in the suburbs. I go to church every Sunday. I haven't had a drop to drink since that night and have no desire for the stuff. Anyway, I wanted to let you know what a difference you've made in my life. You were a friend to this sorry, good-for-nothing, homeless guy who'd lost all hope."*

James laid his hand on Danny's shoulder and said, *"That's the reason I came tonight—to tell you that what you're doing is very important. I'm just one example of how important it is. Thanks for helping me see the truth. Thanks for being my friend. You helped me more than you know and now I'm going to do the same for others. I have a two-bedroom apartment and I'm going to take in a homeless guy and help him change. I'm going to do for someone else what you did for me."*

Unhindered tears flowed down Danny's face. James reached in his pocket and handed Danny a check, *"I have a small gift for you. It's my way of saying thanks. I know it's not much, but it's all I have."*

Danny looked at the $25.00 check and was speechless. James put his arm around Danny's shoulder laughed and said, *"Don't worry, it's good."*

They both laughed. The two men embraced as Danny replied, *"Thanks so much, James. You have no idea how much I needed to be encouraged. Today's been a really difficult day, but you just changed all that. You just blessed my socks off, brother."*

* * * * * * * * * * *

Just in case you were wondering, the check cleared the bank.

We saw James a few months later. He had a friend with him. True to his word, he'd taken in a homeless man and both were doing very well.

CHAPTER TEN

It's Worth It All

Therefore, my beloved brethren, be steadfast, immovable,
Always abounding in the work of the Lord,
Knowing that your toil is not in vain in the Lord.
I Corinthians 15:58

It matters not...
if you preach to one or to ninety.
It matters not...
if you're the one who reaps the harvest.
It matters only....
That you sew along your path the
precious love of your Savior.

It was Thursday night and our team once again headed to the inner city. It was obvious we were all exhausted. Our conversation consisted of complaining, moaning, and groaning. It went from bad to worse when we began questioning why we even bothered ministering to the homeless. Were we really accomplishing anything or were we just wasting our time?

Thoughts of turning around and never coming back were beginning to sound quite appealing. With no hope of coming out of this slump on our own, someone wisely suggested we pray. Our prayers seemed like nothing more than empty words. Finally, someone prayed, *"Lord, we are in desperate need of encouragement and tonight wouldn't be too soon."*

We rode the rest of the way in silence. We arrived, unloaded the van and had just begun handing out the meals, when I noticed a police car making its usual rounds. I looked at my watch, he was right on time. I half-heartedly waved and he waved back. Instead of continuing on as usual, he stopped his car in the middle of the street, stepped out and motioned for me to come to him.

My negative attitude immediately went into high gear as I said to myself, *"Oh, great! This is exactly what we need tonight. I bet he's going to tell us we have to move to another location. There's probably some new ordinance that forbids feeding people in this park. This is just great!"*

Needless to say, I wasn't in a good frame of mind. I turned to Barbara and said, *"I'll be right back, I hope."*

With a plastic smile on my face, I walked over and greeted the police officer. Thankfully, he didn't seem to notice my attitude but greeted me warmly, then said, *"I have a young man in the back seat that I caught trying to break into a car. I've spent the last hour talking with him and it's my opinion jail isn't the place for him. I believe, what he really needs is someone who'll show him some kindness and understanding. Someone who'll help him get back on his feet and start over. I couldn't think of a better place to bring him than to you guys. Will you help him?"*

That wasn't at all what I expected! I shook my head trying to clear my thoughts, then responded, *"Well, sure. Yeah, we can do that."*

The police officer replied, *"I knew you'd help. Thanks so much."*

As the young man got out of the car, the full impact of what had just happened hit me. This officer, who we'd never met, had brought this young man to us. Why us? We'd never spoken; the only connection he'd had with us was the Thursday night wave as he drove by, week after week, month after month, and year after year. We were there in the bitter cold and the scorching heat. We offered cold drinks and hot meals to some homeless people. We brought them clothing and blankets. We laughed with them and cried with them. We listened to their stories, some true and some not. We prayed with them. That's all he knew about us. Without us saying one word, he'd been impacted.

Needless to say my spirits soared! In that moment, I went from total discouragement to incredible elation!

I introduced myself to the young man as we sat on the curb. Danny brought him a plate of food, which he laid aside. He said, *"My name's Stephen and my father's a pastor. A really good pastor, I might add. I gave my life to Jesus at six-years-old. When I was fifteen, I started hanging out with some guys that were the partying kind. I soon found myself thinking I needed to stretch my wings and do things my way for a change. I found myself hating my dad's rules. I decided I wanted to have some fun. Soon after my 17th birthday I ran away from home and God. I've been running ever since looking for fun and excitement. Believe me, I found some but what I mostly found was trouble and heartache. When you're running from God, there's only one way to go and that's down. I found myself in the bottom of a pit and you know what? It didn't take me long to realize I didn't like it. Just this morning, sitting under a bridge watching the sunrise, I realized just how far from God I was and it scared me. I thought back to the peace and contentment I used to have. I missed going to bed at night and not feeling guilty. I missed my mom and dad. So, for the first time in a couple of years, I prayed. I told God I was tired of running and asked for a second chance. I asked Him to send someone to help me. From the looks of things I think He's answered my prayer."*

I replied, *"Stephen, we've been feeding people in this park every week for several years. But tonight, we were all tired and very discouraged. We felt like it didn't matter if we came here or not because we hadn't seen very much fruit from our efforts. I want to tell you that **you** are an answer to **our** prayers as well. God heard your prayer this morning; He heard ours less than two hours ago and brought us all together. I'm really glad to meet you, Stephen."*

That night, we drove Stephen to a discipleship house where he was received with open arms. With each report, we learned that

Stephen was doing exceptionally well. As a matter of fact, he was doing so well that just three months later he was reunited with his family. The prodigal son went home.

* * * * * * * * * *

If for just one—it's worth it all.

Part III

HIS MARVELOUS WAYS

THE MIRACLE WORKER

He's the great miracle worker.
Healing a withered hand, on the Sabbath.
He's the great miracle worker.
Spitting on the eyes of a blind man, restoring his vision.

He's the great miracle worker.
Casting out a demon, healing a boy.
He's the great miracle worker.
Cleansing *ten* leprous men, and *one* returns to thank Him.

He's the great miracle worker.
Providing the temple taxes, from the mouth of a fish.
He's the great miracle worker.
Feeding a hungry multitude with five loaves and two fish.

He's the great miracle worker.
Raising the son of a widow with just a touch of the coffin.
He's the great miracle worker
Stretching out His hand—He calms the angry sea.

He's the great miracle worker
Yesterday, today and tomorrow—healing, delivering and
restoring.
And He's still the great miracle worker
Among the destitute,
Among the rich,
Among you,
And me.

CHAPTER ELEVEN

The Green Army Blanket

The Lord also will be a stronghold for the oppressed,
A stronghold in times of trouble.
And those who know Thy name will put their trust in Thee;
For Thou, O Lord, hast not forsaken those who seek Thee.
Psalm 9:9-10

HOMELESS
Wandering in the dark,
Shivering from the cold,
Looking for a safe haven,
Wondering if anyone cares?

In Kansas City, alone, more than 400 people sleep on the streets *every* night.

𝕴 heard footsteps before I saw anyone. It was much too dark in Jurassic Park to see clearly. One of our volunteers called out to the footsteps, *"Are you hungry? Would you like a bowl of chili?"*

A man answered, *"Yes, ma'am, I'd be much obliged."*

It was his southern drawl that got my attention. He stepped into the dim light. He looked to be about 30 years old. His overalls were dirty and so was his jacket. His hat wasn't any better. And as for his shoes, well, they hardly qualified to be called shoes.

It wasn't his outward appearance that troubled me most, even though I was concerned that his clothing wasn't warm enough for our freezing temperatures. But, what really disturbed me was the deep sadness etched on his face. He appeared to be carrying the weight of the world on his sagging shoulders. I knew that look. That was the look of a broken heart, a crushed spirit.

Extending my hand, I said, *"Hi, my name's Rhonda. I couldn't help but notice your southern accent. I'm from Georgia, where are you from?"* He shook my hand as if I was a long lost relative and smiled warmly. He answered, *"My name's Brian and I'm from Georgia same as you."*

We talked about several different places in Georgia we both were familiar with as Barbara handed him a steaming bowl of chili. Warming his hands on the chili bowl, he quickly consumed the food. I asked what brought him to Kansas City. He laid down his bowl and answered, *"Well, my wife ran off with another man and took my baby girl with her. I don't know where they are now. After a few weeks of grievin' I just couldn't take it anymore and walked out on my job. I hitched me a ride on a train, not caring where it took me. That was about two months ago and here I am in the middle of the coldest cold I've ever known.*

Last night, I was walkin' the streets tryin' to find a place to get warm. The later it got, the colder I got. I got worried I might freeze to death. Then, I remembered what my grandma said. If she said it once, she said it a thousand times, 'Now sonny, whenever you find yourself in trouble, the first thing you gotta do is tell the good Lord all about it, then trust Him to lead you out of your trouble. God will always take care of you.'

I've been a Christian since I was a boy and never would've thought I'd ever walk away from the Lord. But I tell ya, when my wife ran off, I got mad at her and God and everybody. I figured God must not care about me one little bit, so I just ran away and I've been runnin' ever since.

Last night, I came to my senses and got down on my knees on this frozen ground and prayed. I told the Lord all about what happened with my wife and how I ran away, too. I told Him I was real sorry and asked Him to forgive me. I also asked for a warm place to sleep. Then, I got up and just started walking. I walked a couple blocks, not really payin' attention to where I was goin' when all of a sudden I noticed a building. It had a covered loadin' dock, so I hurried on over there. Well, you ain't ever seen a man more happy as I was when I found a green army blanket crumpled up on that there ledge. Since nobody was around, I figured it was free for the takin'. Wasting no time, I wrapped it around me and curled up in the corner. But before I went to sleep, I thanked the Lord for my grandma and for leading me to this place where a blanket was waitin' for me. Then I fell asleep.

Sometime later, a sharp pain in my side woke me up. I jumped up ready to defend myself. Standing in front of me was a little old man with a walking stick. His stick was poised, ready to give me another good whack. He said, 'That's my blanket you got there. You ain't gonna steal my blanket!'

I quickly unwrapped myself from the blanket and handed it to him saying, 'I'm sorry, I wasn't tryin' to steal your blanket. I didn't know it belonged to anybody.'

He relaxed, lowered his stick and asked, 'Ain't you got one of your own?'

'No sir. I was freezin' to death, so I prayed for a warm place to sleep and I happened on this place; that's when I saw this blanket. But I didn't know it was yours.'

Well, that ole fella' leaned back on his stick and said, 'Since you ain't got a blanket and I got two, you can use it for tonight. Just be sure and leave it here in the morning.'

He gave me the blanket, then climbed up the steps and laid down. Tell ya the truth, I was kinda glad for the company. That man's kindness kept me warm last night. But, I ain't sure what I'm gonna do tonight. I figure God's gonna take care of me just like He did last night."

By now, I was quite excited, *"Brian, I believe God led you to that green army blanket last night and I believe He led you here tonight. Just like He took care of you last night, He's going to take care of you tonight. What you don't know is that we come here every Thursday night and give away clothes, coats and blankets. You're definitely in the right place at the right time. We'll give you a blanket and a coat. We even have some really warm socks for you, too. But first, let's get you some more chili."*

Brian hadn't eaten in two days, so he had a healthy appetite. When he couldn't eat another bite, we took him to the van to pick out a coat. He tried on several, finally finding one that fit his very muscular frame. Next, we brought out a box filled with beautiful, new blankets. But, Brian pointed in the back of the van and asked, *"Can I have that one?"*

Folded under the seat was a very old, green army blanket that I'd put there weeks before thinking no one would want it.

Brian left that night with some extra food, a new coat, two pairs of socks, a green army blanket securely tucked under his arm, and a big smile on his face.

* * * * * * * * * *

Two weeks later, an excited Brian told us he'd found a job as a chef's apprentice in a dinner club. Several months passed before we saw him again. He looked great! His clothes were neat and clean. He had on new shoes and a nice hat. He said he loved his job and was doing really well. He lived in a one-room apartment. The best thing was that he no longer carried the weight of the world on his shoulders.

That night, when Brian turned to leave he said, *"By the way, I sleep under that army blanket every night. That's one blanket I figure I'll keep forever because it reminds me to run **to** God and not **from** Him. It also reminds me, I can trust God to take care of little ole me."*

Amen to that.

CHAPTER TWELVE

The Never Ending Chili

For nothing will be impossible with God.
Luke 1:37

There are times when God intervenes in dramatic ways,
Reminding us that impossible things
for us are always possible for Him!

𝕴 woke to a bitter, cold February day and my thoughts immediately focused on my homeless friends. I decided to make a large pot of chili to take downtown that night. It was my feeble attempt to provide them with a little warmth.

Later that day, Jenny, one of the volunteers called and asked, *"What're we taking to the street tonight?"*

"I have a pot of chili cooking right now."

She replied, *"I'll bring a pot, too."*

"We probably won't need it, but go ahead and make it and if we don't use it we'll just freeze it."

By evening, the temperature had dropped to ten degrees, but with the wind chill factor it was minus twenty-two degrees. Being raised in southern Georgia, I find it nearly impossible to dress warm enough. I put on numerous layers of clothes and a very puffy, white snowsuit. The end result was that the homeless and many on our team lovingly referred to me as the Pillsbury dough-girl.

That night, we had two very large pots of chili. We set up the tables and within minutes a long line of people were waiting for something hot to fill their empty stomachs. Where had they all come from? Normally, when it's this cold we have only a handful of homeless people join us for dinner because they find the warmest place possible and won't leave it because someone will claim it.

Jenny and I filled bowl after bowl with chili. In less than half an hour, my pot was empty and Jenny had about two inches of chili in hers. I knew we were in trouble. The number of people in line was even more now than when we began. There was no way we'd have enough.

I leaned over to Jenny and said, *"My pot's empty. Start praying, we're going to run out of chili."*

With every ladle of chili Jenny served, we asked God to multiply it. I watched several people come around the corner and get in line. Others came back and asked if they could have seconds. With very little faith I answered, *"We don't have much left, but you can get back in line and try."*

The thoughts of turning away even one hungry person fueled our prayers.

Jenny and I were thrilled beyond words as those who got back in line for seconds held out their bowls for more and we actually had some to give them. We told them this was nothing short of a miracle and they commented that this was the best chili they'd ever had. Several said, it was so good we should can it to sell. We'd never had so many compliments about our food.

An hour later, we were still dipping from the smaller pot. The last person was served, everyone was full and the last man headed to his 'bed' under a nearby bridge. Jenny and I looked at the bottomless pot. There was about four inches of chili left! There had been only about two inches when we started praying. We knew we were looking at a miracle! There was absolutely **no way** the small amount of chili in that pot could've fed so many people! No way, except for the fact that God loves those precious people so much that He not only multiplied our chili, but also improved it—just for them.

* * * * * * * *

Jenny and I witnessed a miracle that night. Our faith was stretched just as that chili was. And a large number of very cold, homeless people ate chili that came straight from heaven's recipe. No wonder they bragged about it so much.

CHAPTER THIRTEEN

Keep Reaching

Do nothing from selfishness or empty conceit,
but with humility of mind
Let each of you regard one another
as more important than himself;
Do not merely look out for your own personal interests,
But also for the interests of others.
Philippians 2:3-4

'Sacrifice'—it's almost a forbidden word in our society.
Yet, it's the very heart of Christianity.

It was mid January and there were only five of us crazy enough to face our record-breaking temperature. Our homeless friends sat huddled together beside the outside wall of the homeless shelter. They'd sleep on the sidewalk tonight, if they managed to get warm enough that is. All of the area homeless shelters were filled to capacity, as usual.

We opened the van doors and they hurried over to us. Within a few minutes, each person held steaming cups of cocoa or coffee in their frozen hands, while we hurried to set out the food.

It wasn't long before the meals were eaten and the trash collected. Then, we announced we had blankets for anyone who didn't have one and a line quickly formed. I climbed into the back seat of the van and passed the blankets to Mary Lee who handed them out of the van to the next person in line.

Everything was going smoothly, until Mary Lee noticed a man get in line for the second time. She said, *"I'm sorry, but we can't give you another blanket. Because we have so few we've asked that each person only get one."*

"But I gotta' have another blanket!" He said rather adamantly.

"I'm sorry, but..." Mary Lee responded.

"I've got six kids and they're cold. I want another blanket!"

He refused to listen as we explained there was only one per person. The more he talked, the more obvious it became that he was either drunk, high, or both. Mary Lee and I looked at each other not quite sure how to handle this rare occurrence. I remembered a very old and ragged blanket that was under the seat. Perhaps that would satisfy him. Mary Lee handed it to him, hoping he'd leave. It worked, but a few minutes later the man returned and broke in front of the line demanding another blanket. We absolutely refused and told him we wouldn't pass out another blanket as long as he was standing there. Seeing that we meant business, he stepped aside. But, as soon as we handed out the next blanket he snatched it from the lady's arms and ran off with it. I watched him unlock the trunk of a parked car and throw this blanket on top of the other two. Not only did he now have three blankets, but he also had a car and perhaps even a nice warm house!

I told myself that he wouldn't get another blanket. We had about twenty blankets left and the line was still quite long so I said, *"Mary Lee, we're going to run out before everyone gets one."*

Latisha, the women next in line heard me, so when Mary Lee handed her a blanket she said, *"I'll just wait until last and if you have a blanket left I'll take one then. If not, that's okay."*

"But, there are more people in line than we have blankets. If you need one, you really should take this one."

Latisha replied, *"Really, it's okay. I'll wait."*

Mary Lee and I were deeply touched, especially after experiencing the man who took three blankets.

Latisha said, *"I'll just wait right here. I'd be glad to help you pass them out if you want."*

I answered, *"Great, you're hired."*

Latisha climbed in the van and went right to work. Almost immediately, we heard a disturbance and looked up just in time to see the man with three blankets pushing a woman out of his way, so that he was first in line. He demanded, *"Give me another blanket."*

I leaned forward and said, *"You already have three and there's no way we're going to give you another."*

He was furious and jumped into the van. I saw the fire of hate in his eyes and knew I was in trouble. I sent up a quick *"Help, Lord!"* and at the same time looked out the window for Danny. He was much too far away to hear if I called. The raging man was still trying to get to me. I was about to be hurt, probably seriously. In that instant, Latisha positioned her rather large body between him and me, cutting off his advance. Putting her finger in his face, she said, *"Back off, boy!"*

He tried pushing her aside, but she didn't budge. She continued, *"Just who do you think you are and just what do you think you're doin'? This here is a woman of God and there's no way under God's blue sky I'm going to let you touch her! You got that, boy?"*

Still livid, he lunged against her.

Latisha braced herself against the seat and very sternly said, *"I told you to **back off!**"*

He looked first at her, then at me. His eyes were filled with hatred and evil. It seemed as if time had stopped. I whispered, *"The angel of the Lord encamps around those who fear Him, and rescues them."* (Psalm 34:7).

Once more Latisha said, *"I said for you to back off, **now!**"*

Giving her one last shove, he backed out of the van then got in his car. I relaxed, but only after he drove out of sight.

Trying to calm my racing heart, I turned my attention to Latisha and said, *"Thanks for your help."*

"No problem," she said.

"I'm just curious, how did you know I'm a Christian?"

"That's easy, nobody in their right minds would come down here in this kind of cold for folks like us. Nobody, that is except

somebody like Jesus. So, the way I figure it that means you must be a Christian."

I was blessed.

Now that the excitement was over, we began handing out the blankets again. We soon had only two blankets left; I counted the people in line, there were ten.

I handed Mary Lee a blanket and said, *"There's only one left."*

"Multiply the blankets, Lord," we prayed.

I reached for the last blanket and gave it to Mary Lee. Sadness swept over me knowing we were going to send eight people away empty-handed. I picked up an empty box that was on the seat beside me and threw it in the back. In doing so, I saw that there was now a blanket where there wasn't one a few minutes ago! Excitedly, I grabbed it and handed it to Mary Lee who handed it to Latisha. I could tell by the look on their faces that they were just as surprised as I was.

I said, *"Don't ask, just keep praying. I don't have the faith to look, but I do have the faith to keep reaching."*

That's exactly what I did. I reached behind me until I felt the softness of a blanket, then handed it to Mary Lee, who handed it to Latisha, who gave it to a very cold person. After the fifth blanket, we were beside ourselves with joy! We knew beyond a shadow of a doubt that we were experiencing the supernatural provision of God.

Just when we were down to two people, four more homeless women got in line. Finally, the last person walked away with a blanket wrapped around her shoulders. What a relief! Every single person got a blanket that night. We were finished, or so I thought until I looked at Latisha and remembered her willingness to give up her blanket for the benefit of another.

Latisha had a pleasant face, beautiful skin and bright eyes. She actually looked quite peaceful and happy, which is very rare among the homeless. What a blessing she'd been, especially to me!

Just then, Mary Lee looked at me. I knew she was thinking the same thing. I whispered one last prayer, took a very deep breath and said, *"Here goes."*

I reached behind me without looking and felt only stiff plastic. Puzzled, I turned to see what it was. There, under my hand, was a plastic zippered bag. It took both of my hands to lift it. Inside was a beautiful quilt, which I handed to Latisha.

She clapped her hands and tried unsuccessfully to dance inside the van as she said, *"Oh, thank you, thank you, thank you! It's so beautiful. It's the best of them all!"*

"I agree. God saved the best for last and I'm talking about you, Latisha. You're the best!"

We got out of the van to admire her handmade quilt. It truly was beautiful. Soon, it was time to go, so we bid Latisha farewell and loaded the back of the van with our tables, drinks, and other supplies. There were absolutely no blankets there. When we arrived home, Danny found three more blankets folded neatly on top of our supplies. Where they came from was anybody's guess. My vote is they came straight from heaven.

* * * * * * * * * *

Sadly, I never saw Latisha again. But, you can be sure I won't ever forget her.

CHAPTER FOURTEEN

The Hot Dog Story

Every good thing bestowed and every perfect gift is from above,
Coming down from the Father of lights,
With whom there is no variation, or shifting shadow.
James 1:17

An elderly lady once told me her
secret for living a fulfilled life.
She said, *"Pray as if it depends on God
and work as if it depends on you."*

𝕴t had been one of those weeks when everything that can go wrong does. I'd been running non-stop and was very glad it was Friday. My husband, Danny, was very sick and confined to bed. I said good-bye to him, then raced to my morning prayer meeting.

I pulled onto the highway and tuned into the world around me. The sun was bright and the sky was clear; maybe today would be a better day. I noticed beautiful wildflowers growing on the side of the road dancing to music only they could hear. I drank in the beauty that surrounded me and peace flooded my weary soul. I thanked the Lord for such beauty, then began to go over my schedule with Him. In doing so, I realized I'd forgotten to buy the hot dogs for the youth meeting at my house that evening. There was absolutely no time to make a trip to the grocery store, so I prayed,

"Lord, would You provide the hot dogs for tonight and would You have them delivered to my house?"

Trusting He'd heard my plea and would come to my aid, I continued on with my prayer.

Later that evening, I rushed home to prepare for the youth that would be arriving within the hour. I thought of the hot dogs. *"Lord, I really needed your help on this one,"* I mumbled as I walked to my bedroom.

"Danny, you'll have to let everyone in, I have to make a trip to the grocery store for hot dogs."

Danny answered, *"You don't have to go. Sally called and asked if we could use a case of hot dogs. I told her we most certainly could. She was really excited and even offered to drop them off on her way home from work. She should be here anytime now."*

In a matter of minutes the doorbell rang. My prayer had been answered as Sally walked in with a very large box. Curious, I said, *"I just have to know how this whole thing happened. Why did you call us and where did you get so many hot dogs?"*

"I work at a meat packaging plant. Just before quitting time, there was a weird glitch and all these hot dogs come through without wrappers and then the machine shut down. My supervisor asked if anyone wanted them, but no one did, including me. I'm tired of hot dogs, eight long hours, five days a week of nothing but hot dogs. No way did I want them. Anyway, when I was clocking out, I felt someone tap me on the shoulder. I turned around to respond, but no one was there. That's when the thought came to me that you guys might be able to use them. So, here I am."

That night, I went to bed thinking about what a wonderful day it had been. I marveled at God's wonderful ways. The God of the universe had heard my prayer and cared about something as insignificant as hot dogs. My imagination went into high gear as I thought about what might have taken place in heaven that day.

I pictured my prayer taking wings and soaring like an arrow through heaven's gate. It heads straight for the Throne Room where the awesome hand of God captures my little plea. He embraces it and it becomes His. Then, with a voice like the sound of many waters, He summons an angel named Oscar. The sound fills all of heaven, then spills out into eternity.

With utmost haste, Oscar kneels before the great Throne.

The Lord speaks, but this time in a still, small voice. *"Oscar, I have a high priority, important assignment for you. There's a meat packaging plant in Kansas City and I want you to go there. When you arrive, this is what you are to do...."*

Oscar turns to leave. He steps through the Great Doors and once he's in the Grand Hall exclaims, *"Hot dog! I'm going to Kansas City!"*

Retrieving his backpack from his locker, he pulls out an abacus and begins his calculations. After quite a lengthy time and much frustration, he gives up and returns to the Throne Room to wait for another audience with the King of all kings.

Even though Oscar's been in this room many times, he's still overwhelmed. In front of him is the Throne of God and sitting on it is the One and only true God clothed in unspeakable glory. An emerald rainbow fills the space over Him. Bolts of lightning and peals of thunder explode from the heart of the Throne and fill the room. The floor is a sea of glass—like the finest crystal. On this sea are seven lamp stands holding seven lamps. Each lamp contains fire that burns before the Holy God continually and standing in the midst of those lamps is the Son of God, the Lamb who was slain for the sins of the world! This One is clothed in a robe reaching His feet and a pure gold belt encircles His waist. His head and His hair are white like virgin snow. His eyes are like a flame of fire. His feet are like brass, glowing in an oven. And His face—oh, what a face! It shines brighter than the sun at high noon. Who can look on that wonderful face and stand? Oh, there is none like Him to be found in heaven or on earth!

Oscar falls to his knees. Around him are thousands upon thousands of angels saying with a loud voice, *"Worthy is the Lamb that was slain, to receive power and riches and wisdom and might and honor and glory and blessing."*

Oscar eagerly joins their worship. Closing his eyes, Oscar is immediately swept away in adoration. All thoughts are lost, except for thoughts of the King. And, then, without warning, the sound of thunder explodes from the Throne as Oscar's name is once more called. Startled, Oscar's rather over-sized wings spring out like a jackknife knocking himself and the angel Gertrude on their faces. Quite a commotion follows as Oscar tries to disentangle his wings from Gertrude's. Finally, Oscar manages to stand. He then reaches down to help Gertrude back to her feet. With an innocent smile and raised eyebrows Oscar says, *"You're not too sturdy today, hey Gertie?"*

With a most frustrated look, Gertie smoothes the creases from her wings and replies, *"Oscar, I was doing quite fine until you knocked me over."*

Gertrude looks at Oscar and is perplexed at the willingness of the Creator to choose weak, clumsy, imperfect vessels to do His bidding—just one of the many mysteries that surrounds this King.

Oscar tucks his wings securely in place and then proceeds to the Throne of God. He kneels before the One who sees and knows all things and says, *"Lord, I'm just an angel and quite limited in my understanding of Your awesome ways. I know that You're generous and that You're able to do exceedingly, abundantly beyond all a person could ask or think. Keeping that in mind, I'm not exactly sure how to calculate 'exceedingly, abundantly' in hot dogs. Just how many is that, Lord?"*

The Lord smiles at this angel before Him. He looks directly into the center of his being and knows He's chosen wisely, for this one has a strong desire to please his Maker. His heart more than makes up for his blunders.

The Lord speaks, *"Oscar, Rhonda needs six pounds of hot dogs, so let Us give her seventy pounds. Oscar, remember to follow your instructions exactly. This is vital for you to succeed."*

With his dilemma resolved, Oscar skips past Gertrude and winks. She shakes her head in disbelief. Oscar quickly exits the Pearly Gates and hurries toward earth.

As he travels through time and space, in a voice quite off-key, he sings, *"Goin' to Kansas City. Kansas City, here I come! They got a whole lot of hot dogs there and I'm gonna get Rhonda some."*

Within seconds, he arrives in earth's atmosphere and immediately comes to a stop. He's overwhelmed by this creation. Since the beginning of creation, humanity's been a deep mystery to him. Oscar's spent thousands of years and numerous hours pondering the unique relationship between God and man. It's a relationship much deeper than the relationship between God and the angelic host. Lost in thought, he doesn't notice the angel who has come up behind him. This angel lays his hand on Oscar's shoulder, and as usual, Oscar is startled. His over-sized, unruly wings fly out and slam right into Meyer, who fortunately was prepared. Apologizing profusely, he tucks his wings back in place. Not believing he'd nearly knocked over his supervisor, he mumbles, *"I'm such a misfit. I'm so clumsy and these over-grown wings of mine constantly get me in trouble. Sometimes I wonder why the Creator even keeps me around. As for these wings, well, I think I'd be better off without them."*

Oscar plops down on a nearby cloud, propping his chin in his hands.

The angel, Meyer, comes alongside him and says, *"Oscar, if you didn't have your wings then you couldn't fly. And, if you couldn't fly, then you wouldn't be able to do what God asks of you, could you?"*

"Well—no, I guess I couldn't."

"And, if you couldn't do what God asked, why, you'd be the most miserable angel in all of heaven, wouldn't you?"

Oscar nods.

"Oscar, don't worry so much about being perfect. God never expects perfection. He only expects you to worship Him and out of that adoration to serve Him. It's that simple. And, that's exactly what you're doing. Therefore, don't be so hard on yourself, my friend."

His words wash away Oscar's secret shame. He knows he'll never be perfect, but he certainly adores his Creator and loves to serve Him. And, if that's good enough for God, then it's good enough for him.

Taking a deep breath, Oscar turns his attention back to earth. Meyer is the first to speak. *"It's quite a Masterpiece, is it not?"*

Oscar nods in agreement. He and Meyer talk of the unconditional love that the Godhead has for mankind. No other created being has the privilege of being loved like this. Sure, God cares about the angels along with all His creation, but the love the Father, Son and Holy Spirit has for man is different. It's a love that cost everything. A price the angels could never understand. To think that the Father allowed mere mortal men to crucify His beloved Son is more than they could comprehend. On that day, every angel in heaven was eager and ready to deliver Jesus from the hands of men! Yet, the God of the universe remained silent while all of heaven watched His Son suffer and die. And on earth, the Son of God never once cried out for help. Instead, He allowed mere men to nail his hands and feet to a cross—all because of His great love for them.

Oscar turns to Meyer and asks, *"Do they not understand, do they not know how much He loves them?"*

Meyer responds, *"I don't believe many of them do. But, Oscar, be assured of this one thing—the mystery still unfolds. Before the end of time, all of earth will surely know. Then, every knee will bow and every tongue will say that Jesus is Lord."*

Meyer's words bring comfort to Oscar as he has a strong desire for mankind to know the incredible love of Jesus.

Meyer, being sent to make certain Oscar fulfills his mission asks, *"So, Oscar aren't you on your way to Kansas City?"*

"Oh, yeah, I almost forgot. I've got to get some hot dogs."

Bidding each other Godspeed, Oscar resumes his journey. Within moments, he arrives at the meat packing plant and makes his way to the assembly line. From his backpack, he pulls out a scale and weighs each hot dog. *"The Lord said 70 pounds and that's exactly what the Lord will have."*

He carefully weighs the hot dogs and quite creatively sneaks them onto the conveyor belt. He removes a bolt from the wrapping machine and puts it in his backpack. Having accomplished his task, he strolls through the plant looking at the men and women busy at work, the majority living their lives with no regard to eternity. *"Oh, if only they knew what awaits them on the other side,"* Oscar whispers, *"then they'd live so differently."*

He hears a noise behind him and sees Sally leaving. *"Oh, no, she can't leave! Not yet,"* he exclaims.

Oscar runs across the large room and overshoots his mark. Losing his balance, he falls on his buns, slides past Sally and finally comes to rest against a large freezer door. With no time to waste, he jumps up and decides it would be better and less painful to fly. His wings arrive before he does and one of them brushes Sally's shoulder causing her to turn around. Perfect, he leans forward and whispers, *"Call Danny and Rhonda—they need those hot dogs and offer to deliver them."*

It worked; she heard him!

Sally loads the seventy pounds of hot dogs into her pick-up truck, while Oscar dances a jig in the parking lot. Wanting to see his mission to its completion, Oscar follows Sally to Rhonda's door. Oscar unleashes his over-sized wings to pat himself on the back then looks up to heaven and says, *"This one's for You, Lord."*

A peal of thunder shakes the earth as the creator says, *"Well done, Oscar."* Gertie looks down and shakes her head in amazement.

* * * * * * * *

I fell asleep that night secure in the fact that God really takes good care of me. He helps me with the challenges in my life regardless of how big or small. As for Oscar, he taught me not to worry so much about my blunders and weaknesses because God sees my heart and loves me just the way I am.

The perfect ending to a perfect day.

As for the surplus hot dogs, we took them to a low-income housing project and grilled them for the children there. We had such a good time that we made this a monthly event.

CHAPTER FIFTEEN

A Man of Integrity

Vindicate me, O Lord, for I've walked in my integrity;
And I have trusted in the Lord without wavering.
Psalm 26:1

Jesus paid a debt that wasn't His
And He paid it with His life.

𝕴 met Daniel over five years ago. His blue eyes were overflowing with hurt. He was very quiet and always looked exhausted. It was obvious he was in a great deal of pain. He soon became part of our home group, where I came to know him as a man of integrity. Here's Daniel's story:

> "I'd given my life to the Lord at a young age, but through the years I slowly drifted away from Him. It wasn't a conscious decision or a purposeful act; I just replaced Him with things this world had to offer. I was living my life the way I wanted to live it.
>
> I soon married and thought I'd live happily ever after. I believed if I was a good husband, worked hard, and did what was right everything would be great. God wasn't very important in my life.

*Thankfully, God didn't leave me in that state. He pro-
ceeded to claim what was rightfully His. God came after
me like a lion goes after its prey and that's exactly what I
needed.*

*My wife and I were married for less than a year when
I discovered she was having an affair. At this time, she
was pregnant with my son. I was crushed. I loved her. I
asked her to break off the relationship, but she refused. I
wandered around for weeks not knowing what to do or
where to find the answers to the many questions I had. In
just one moment, my whole world had been turned upside
down. I felt as if I was perpetually falling with no ground
in sight.*

*I desperately needed help, so I turned to my family.
My brothers patiently listened, then reminded me of the
only One who could help me. They pointed me to Jesus.
The intensity of my pain drove me back to the cross where
I fell on my knees in surrender. I began to seek Jesus with
all of my breaking heart. God began putting me back together; He took what Satan meant for evil and used it to
bring me back to Him.*

*Soon after I'd discovered my wife's infidelity, she asked
for a divorce, but the law prohibited it while she was pregnant. I took advantage of this and desperately tried to win
her back. But, in reality it was many nights of coming
home from work, finding a note on the table telling me
leftovers were in the refrigerator and she'd gone to bed
early. Most of the time, I'd find two glasses, two knives,
two forks, and two plates sitting in the sink, evidence of the
dinner she'd enjoyed with another man.*

*Because she didn't care about my future or about me,
she took our credit cards and went on numerous shopping
sprees, unbeknownst to me. She charged clothing, gifts for
her family and boyfriend, evenings out, trips, etc. I was
hurting so deeply that I didn't notice what she was pur-
chasing, nor did I question how she was paying for it, until
it was too late. When I received the bills and saw the*

charges, I immediately cut up all of our cards, but the damage had already been done. I had five credit cards, four of which she'd charged to the limit. I was already paying on my $12,000 school loan plus our monthly living expenses. These new charges put me in serious financial debt. Through it all, I continued to pray for reconciliation.

The months passed and my son was born. It should've been one of the happiest days of my life, but instead it was a time of great confusion. I found myself bouncing back and forth between two dynamics. I was losing someone I loved, but at the same time gaining a precious addition in my life. I grieved over the fact there was no one with whom I could share the joys of fatherhood. At times, the void in my life was unbearable. I loved my new son and decided no matter what did or didn't happen between his mother and I, he'd always know he had a father who loved and cared for him.

Just one month after the birth of my son, my wife divorced me. The morning our divorce was final, I once again asked her to reconsider. Her answer was still no.

Within a short time, she married her boyfriend. I knew it was truly over. I could relate to Humpty Dumpty and his great fall. I knew no one, myself included, would be able to put me back together again. I continued to need God in a desperate way. I was emotionally crushed, spiritually weak, and financially devastated. I cried out to God and He heard me. He gave me the grace to let her go and took me by the hand and walked close by my side. Together, we began the long, hard journey of picking up the broken pieces of my life and putting me back together again.

In the meantime, I had to do something about the wall of debt that was suffocating me. So, I did the only thing I knew to do and that was to take a second job. Six days a week, I worked from 8:00 a.m. to 11:00 p.m.

A few months before my son was born, I met Danny and Rhonda. They were part of a church group that met on Sunday nights, which just happened to be the only night I didn't work. So, I began attending their group. Everyone in the group encouraged, loved, and prayed for me. They surrounded me with hope. I felt like a drowning man who'd finally been thrown a life preserver.

Throughout this difficult time in my life the Lord blessed me tremendously. Many times, I was given groceries because I didn't have anything to eat. Other times, someone would give me money just when I was about to have my utilities disconnected. I was learning to trust God with every detail of my life.

The process of leaning on God to solve my problems and allowing Him to heal my gaping wounds continued. Spiritually, mentally and emotionally things began to get better, but financially I continued to sink. I was made to pay child support that totaled 45% of my 'net' income (I made less then $18,000 a year working two jobs). I was determined to do the right thing and support my son, so I faithfully paid the full amount on time. This left me with very little money to pay the bills I inherited from the marriage.

I continued attending church and pursuing the Lord. I learned the importance of giving and made a commitment to God to tithe each week, regardless of what bills were past due. To this day, I've kept that promise.

For over a year, I continued working two jobs putting in nearly eighty hours each week. The day came when I couldn't do it anymore. I was physically and emotionally exhausted. I quit working my night job and began looking for a better paying day job. Through a series of events, I met a man who told me about a job. It sounded like the very thing I was looking for, so I pursued it. The Lord was with me and I was hired.

My new job was in the computer field and the pay was a little more than my two jobs put together. I've been at this job almost two years now and I love it! In the past two years, I've been given several raises and a promotion, which has been a real blessing.

Even though my financial circumstances haven't changed much, I have. Even with my new job, my debt continues to overwhelm me. I went for financial counseling and was told my only solution was to file bankruptcy. I told the counselor that I'd have to pray before making a decision like that. As I prayed, I felt the Lord say that I was to trust Him and not file for bankruptcy. Consequently, I promised the Lord I'd continue walking out this financial nightmare and trust Him for the solution.

It's been extremely difficult, but I'm learning to trust God on deeper levels. I've learned this life isn't just about doing what's right and being good. That's not enough. I now know I need God more than I need air. And God will take care of all of His children in His way and in His time. He works everything out for our best and according to His purposes.

God hasn't miraculously taken away my pain nor has He erased my debt. But He's faithful to comfort me and to meet my needs. Just last month when I sat down to balance my checkbook, I was more than $400 short. No matter how many times I calculated it, I always came up the same. There was absolutely nothing I could do about it, except trust that the Lord would once again help me.

Several days passed before I sat down to write out the checks, knowing I'd only be able to pay a few of them. I decided which ones I absolutely had to pay and laid the others aside. I wrote checks for the high priority bills and subtracted the money from my bank balance. My calculations showed I still had money in the bank, so I went back over the figures. Not trusting my math, I checked once again. They were accurate. I wrote checks for the rest of my bills and was able to pay every bill with money leftover. I can't explain how this happened. I didn't deposit any money in my account and didn't change any figures in my checkbook from my first calculations. I still don't know how God did that, but I'm sure glad He did. It's nice to know we have a God, who isn't bound by natural laws, but can and does override them when necessary.

Things are still very difficult for me financially. But, spiritually and in every other way things are very good. Living my life with God in the center guarantees that I'll live happily ever after because He's the One who makes me happy. He's all that really matters."

Danny and I watched Daniel walk through that fiery furnace and in the midst of it, he discovered Jesus standing right beside him, protecting him from the flames. Daniel chose to pay his ex-wife's debts and did not file bankruptcy. This wasn't even his debt. However, Daniel picked it up and carried it anyway. Jesus did exactly the same for us. He paid a debt that wasn't His and He paid it with His very life.

Before Daniel told me this story, I dreamed that Daniel was completely surrounded by a stone wall. The wall was approximately two feet thick and extended from floor to ceiling. A great wall of debt imprisoned him. In the dream, the Lord walked up to the outside wall and with one glance, something like a laser beam cut through the wall making a door. He then invited Daniel to come out and walk with Him.

When I woke up, I prayed that the Lord would set Daniel free from his financial prison. I asked the Lord what part Danny and I could play in helping him. Several days later, the idea came to share his story in our monthly newsletter. As a result, there was a tremendous outpouring of love, prayers and financial gifts for Daniel.

The door was cut through the wall and we received the most donations ever, $14,570 in one month! All of his charge cards were paid in full and the remainder was applied to his school loan. I've never been so proud to be a part of the body of Christ as I was that day!

My friend, Mary Lee expressed it best when she said, *"Years ago when tragedy struck everyone rallied around to do whatever they could do to help. For example, if their barn burned down, the community would gather and rebuild it. That's the way it should be. It is exactly what we as a community of believers did for Daniel. He had a tragedy and the body of Christ helped him.*"

Daniel was convinced he'd never marry again because of his great emotional pain and his impossible debt. But, God is the God of redemption and healing. He redeems what's been wasted and restores what's been lost. God has done just that for Daniel.

* * * * * * * * * *

Just three weeks ago, I attended Daniel's wedding. Everything about it was just beautiful. His four-year-old son was the ring bearer. One of Daniel's brothers stood by his side as his best man. Our youngest daughter, Dana, was one of the bridesmaids. My husband, Danny, gave the bride away. As for me, I was the happiest and proudest mother-of-the-bride in all history the day Daniel married our eldest daughter, Misty.

Written for Daniel on his wedding day:

TODAY, WE GIVE YOU OUR DAUGHTER

Today, we give you our daughter.
Hold her close, keep her safe from harm.
She's one of our most prized possessions.
Together, we give her to you.

Today, we give you our daughter.
Take her hand and lead her on
To higher places, to greater things.
In God, we give her to you.

Today, we give you our daughter.
Treasure her above all things,
Let your heart love her like no other.
In faith, we give her to you.

Today, we give you our daughter.
Stand with her through all things,
Seeking God, together, forever.
Lovingly, we give her to you.

Today, we give you our daughter.
And embrace you as our own son.
We'll love and esteem you always.
Wholeheartedly, we give her to you.

CHAPTER SIXTEEN

Helen's African Violet

For God sees not as man sees,
For man looks at the outward appearance,
But the Lord looks at the heart.
I Samuel 16:7

Life is about the heart.

𝕴t happened two mornings ago when Helen, an elderly friend of mine called. From the frantic sound in her voice, I knew something was wrong. *"Rhonda, I just don't know what to do! Three days ago, my African violet got knocked over and dirt went everywhere. I did my best to put the dirt back around my plant, but I don't think I did so well. This morning my violet looks really bad, so bad that I'm afraid it might die. I was wondering if you could come by today and do something to save it."*

I knew this plant well. It was a birthday present from her only daughter, Barbara who had died the year before. Helen had treasured it. When Barbara was diagnosed with cancer and unable to care for her mother, Helen moved into a nursing home. Helen was not only financially poor, but also very lonely. I knew it would be very difficult for me to find the time in my busy day to get by to see her, but I knew how important this plant was to Helen. I took a deep breath and said, *"Helen, I can't promise I can save your plant, but I'll be by sometime this afternoon and have a look."*

That afternoon, my daughter, Dana, and I made our way to Helen's. This was my first house call as a plant doctor, by the way. We walked in her room and found Helen sitting with the sick plant in her lap. I hugged her and she quickly rehearsed the story of how her beloved plant had suffered such a horrible fall. With just one look, I knew this plant was in very serious trouble. The plant was lying on its side with much of its roots exposed. The leaves were drooping and quite shriveled. Just two weeks before, this African violet was beautifully adorned with nine lavender blooms. (The reason I know there were nine blooms was because Helen had me count them numerous times during our visit.) Now, just two weeks later, something that was so healthy and beautiful was now devastated.

Interrupting my thoughts, Helen asked, *"Well, do you think it's going to die?"*

Picking up the flowerpot, I answered, *"I don't know, Helen. It might, but then again, it might not. Only God knows. I'll do all I can, then we'll leave it in God's hands."*

While I examined the plant, Dana sat down beside Helen. Within minutes, Helen had her photo album out and was sharing stories of her life with Dana. As for me, I took a deep breath and went to work. I began by pruning the dead leaves, which improved its appearance, but didn't do a thing for the real problem. Recognizing the critical problem was that the roots were out of the dirt and exposed to air, I carefully lifted the plant from the pot. Making a deep hole in the dirt, I gently placed the roots in the hole, then filled in the dirt around them. Last, but certainly not least, I gave the plant a drink of water. There wasn't anything more I could do, so I placed the plant on the table beside Helen.

Helen noticed right away and interrupted her story to say, *"Oh, it looks better already! I knew you could fix it!"*

Laying my hand on her shoulder I said, *"Now, Helen, I know your plant looks better, but it's still very sick. It might not make it. We'll just have to wait and see. We need to watch it very carefully. Be sure to open your curtain everyday and let the light in. That'll help, but there's one more thing you can do that will help more than anything."*

Her eyes lit up and she asked, *"What is it?"*

"Pray. Be sure and pray for your little plant, it needs it."

"Pray for a plant? Is that allowed?" Helen asked.

It was obvious, she'd never thought of praying for a plant, but neither had I before that day.

Kneeling beside her, I asked, *"Why wouldn't it be allowed? God cares about everything in our lives, the big and the little things. He cares about everything we care about. You care about your plant, right? Okay then, tell God about it."*

Placing the violet in her lap, she said, *"Okay, I'll do it."*

Dana put away Helen's photo albums and we hugged good-bye. Helen said, *"Thank you girls for coming. You made a helpless, old lady very happy today."*

Patting my hand, she whispered, *"You've got a real good girl there."*

I agreed.

As Dana and I hurried to our next appointment, I thought about how that African violet is so much like life. All is going well. Life is filled with sunshine and beauty. The birds are singing and the sky is clear. Suddenly, a storm hits and our comfortable, little world is turned upside-down, bringing pain and devastation. That's when it's critical to have family and friends who will stand with us.

Looking at my watch, I realized it was later than I thought. I'd spent more time with Helen than I'd planned. Why hadn't I just bought Helen another African violet? It would've been faster and definitely much easier, more convenient for me, but what about Helen? I took a deep, calming breath. I'd done the right thing. I'd shown Helen I loved her by coming to her aid and that was what mattered. The fact that it was much later than I needed it to be just didn't matter anymore. I was glad I'd taken the time to help.

With that settled, I turned to my normally very talkative daughter and realized she hadn't said a word since leaving the nursing home. I asked what was going on. She replied, *"Mom, I feel like I wasted my time back there. I didn't do a thing. All I did was sit and look at some pictures. What good was that? I should've stayed and helped dad load the van. At least that would've been productive."*

I replied, *"Dana, let me encourage you not to judge your actions by the degree of difficulty or by the amount of activity they require. But rather, look at what you do through the Lord's eyes, using the same measuring stick He uses. I know you could've spent the day helping your father and at the end of the day you would've been able to look at something and say, 'I did this and I did that.' That's all good, but what was better, being a friend to someone who was in need and lonely or loading a trailer? In this situation, I believe the better thing was being kind and loving to Helen. You can't ever go wrong with being kind. Dana, you know one of my favorite sayings is, '**Use** things and **love** people.' We use things to love people. Well, that African violet was one of those things. We used it to show Helen how much we love her. I worked on the plant and you 'worked' on Helen. We both were doing the same thing, loving a person. Life really is about loving God and loving people. It's not about a career, or doing things. In truth, it's not even about you. It's about Jesus. Invest your life in God and others. Always remember nothing you ever do unto Him is ever wasted—not your time, your energy, your affection, your labor, your gifts, your talents, or your money. Everything is seen and everything is recorded for eternity. After all, love is the best gift we can ever give—just as Jesus perfectly demonstrated."*

Be the time we reached our destination, Dana was her old self again.

Helen's violet received its daily sunshine and prayers, as Helen faithfully watched over it. Two weeks later, it was looking much better and I was feeling quite confident that it was going to make it. I encouraged Helen to continue praying. When I arrived the following Friday, Helen said, *"You'd better check my violet before we go to lunch, it doesn't look so good."*

I couldn't believe my eyes. The leaves were shriveled and brown. What had happened? I lifted the leaves to check the stem and the whole plant came out of the soil in my hand. The roots were completely shriveled and dead. I said, *"Helen, I'm sorry, but it's dead."*

There was a long, painful pause. Finally, Helen shook her head and with tears in her eyes responded, *"Does that mean I should stop praying for it now?"*

I would've laughed, except she looked like a child who'd just lost a puppy and wasn't quite sure what to do about it. I squeezed her hand and answered, *"Yes, Helen, it means you can stop praying for it."*

"Would you take it with you when you go?" Helen asked.

"Sure."

"All I have is two dollars, but I was wondering if I could have another violet? You know my Barb always grew the most beautiful violets and she always made sure I had one growing in my window."

I clearly understood that Helen's love for violets was directly related to her love for her daughter. *"I'll buy you one this week and bring it next Friday,"* I assured her.

In the course of the following week, I went to several stores looking for a violet, but no one had any. Friday, when I arrived for our lunch date, Helen was ready with the question I was dreading, *"Did you bring me a violet?"*

"Helen, I tried my best to find one, but none of the stores have any. Maybe it's because it's fall; it may be a while before I can find one."

She was clearly disappointed, but graciously tried to hide it.

That afternoon, on my way home, this unsolicited question interrupted my thoughts, *"Why don't you give Helen one of your violets?"*

No way was I going to give away one of my violets! Of all my houseplants, my two violets were my pride and joy. I'd raised them from sprigs and after much loving attention, they were incredibly healthy and covered with beautiful lavender blooms. I quickly squelched that ridiculous suggestion. But it wasn't so easy to avoid in the days ahead. When I'd least expect it, I'd hear that not-so-gentle question, *"Why don't you give her one of your violets?"*

By the second week, I had quite a long list of reasons why I shouldn't give Helen my plant. I held tightly to my idol.

The following weekend, Danny and I visited our good friends, Paul and Lydia. As Lydia and I sat on the porch, she asked about Helen's plant. I answered, *"Sadly, her plant died and I've been unsuccessful in replacing it. For the past two weeks, I've heard this little voice suggesting I give Helen one of mine. Well, I devised a long list of reasons why I didn't have to give up my plant. But just this morning, I realized how selfish I've been. I told the Lord I'd give her one of my plants as soon as we get back home. It's really scary how something as simple as a potted plant had such a strong hold on me. The truth is, this whole thing really wasn't about the plant anyway. It was about my heart and God. In His great love for me, He revealed what was hidden ever so well in my heart. It sure feels good to be free and I can hardly wait to give it away."*

A few hours later, Danny and I went to Wal-Mart. I shopped in one part of the store and he in another. As I headed for the checkout, Danny walked towards me with a big grin on his face. He asked, *"Guess what I found? Do you think Helen would want this even though it's kind of small?"*

I couldn't believe my eyes! From behind his back, he held out a tiny African violet in a cute, little pot complete with a scalloped rim. I examined the plant closer. It was small, but looked strong and healthy. How? Where had he found it? He hadn't heard my conversation that morning with Lydia and he knew I'd given up the search. *"How, where did you find it? And why did you even bother looking in Wal-Mart?"*

He answered, *"I didn't go looking for it. It found me. I was walking by and there it sat in the middle of the aisle on a clearance shelf. I thought of Helen. There was only one, but it looks good and it's marked down to $2.00. Good deal, don't you think?"*

"Better than you know," I replied.

Needless to say, we bought the violet. On the drive home, I looked at the tiny, perfect leaves and wondered at God's mysterious ways. Had He been waiting for me to be willing to give away my violet, not so much concerned about the plant, but deeply concerned about the flaw He saw in my heart? I believe that's exactly what He was doing.

I arrived home and went straight to my violets. They were prominently displayed in my kitchen window and just as beautiful as ever. Their healthy leaves filled their pots and their vibrant blooms made me smile. Thanks to my loving Father, now I could easily give them away. It's amazing how that works.

The following day, I took Helen her baby African violet. She was so surprised and quickly instructed me to clear a place for it on her table. She was so happy and excitedly said, *"Please open the curtains, I'm sure it needs some light. Do you think it needs water? That pot's really small. Do you still have the old one? Perhaps, we should wait a few weeks and then we can re-pot it. Oh, I'm just so happy to have another plant! It feels like home in here again."*

"You're right, Helen, it sure does feel good in here."

* * * * * * * *

Helen's new violet thrived under her attentive care. Several months later, she told me the reason her plant was doing so well was that she'd been praying for it. As for my violets, just a short time after we found the violet in Wal-Mart, I heard about a lady who was going through a very difficult time. I happily gave her one of my plants, and I didn't even flinch.

I learned that idols come in surprising shapes and sizes.

Helen (on the left) with her daughter, Barbara.

Part IV

HEROES OF THE FAITH

THE FOOLISH THINGS

"But God has chosen the foolish things
of the world to shame the wise,
And God has chosen the weak things of the world
To shame the things which are strong,
And the base things of the world and
the despised God has chosen,
The things that are not, so that He might
nullify the things that are,
That no man may boast before God."
I Corinthians 1: 27-29

SERVANTS OF THE KING

Common men,
Common women,
Living uncommon lives
For the sake of the gospel.

Common men
And common women
Dressed in poor men's clothes.
Awaiting the day they wear His robe
And take their place among the heroes of old.
Dressed in His best, washed in His blood—purified.
Children of the King ruling and
reigning throughout eternity.

CHAPTER SEVENTEEN

Barbara's Story

But let it be the hidden person of the heart,
With the imperishable quality of a gentle and quiet spirit,
Which is precious in the sight of God.
I Peter 3:4

Sometimes God says no.

𝕴 met Barbara several years ago. She had a gentleness about her that drew me like a bee to honey. We quickly became close friends. I loved her—that part was easy. Letting her go—that was the difficult part.

Barbara had an inoperable tumor in her body. For eight years, she fought it with everything she had, in every way. This tumor was with her wherever she went. Ever aware of its presence, she learned to live a rich, full life, in spite of it. Barbara rose above it and bloomed. Through it all, she drew ever closer to her Lord and leaned heavily upon Him.

There was a time when it looked as if she was winning the battle against her silent intruder. Her energy increased and she was able to do more than she had in years. Her thin, frail body began to grow stronger and her cheeks grew pink again. But, toward the middle of her last year, it became very painful for Barbara to walk. The tumor was growing. However, that didn't stop her; she continued reaching out to those she loved, which included her weekly visits to her mother, Helen.

Barbara was unable to drive, so I picked her up each Friday and escorted her to the nursing home. I pushed her wheelchair to her mother's room on the second floor. We'd stop several times along the way, so Barbara could talk to the many friends she'd made there. Barbara was a loving person and kind to everyone she met. She quickly became a favorite of the Sisters who operated the home.

The first time I met Barbara's mother, she embraced me with open arms and treated me like one of the family. It was a delight to see how Barbara loved her mother and was so committed to serving her, which she did beautifully.

One Friday, when we arrived for our visit, Helen didn't greet us with her usual cheery greeting. Instead, she tearfully told us she'd broken her favorite necklace the day before and the tiny beads were scattered all over the floor of her room. She was grieved that it was lost forever. Barbara told her mom not to worry, that she'd find the beads. I turned around and saw Barbara on her hands and knees. I knew this must be causing her terrific pain, so I insisted she allow me to pick up the beads. She refused, saying I shouldn't do it because of a back and knee injury I had. That was the kind of woman she was, always thinking of others. So, we both crawled around the room searching for the hundreds of tiny multi-colored beads.

The following Friday, as Barbara was getting into my car, she said, *"I have a real special surprise for my mother today. I can hardly wait to give it to her."*

"What kind of surprise?"

"Oh, you'll have to wait and see," she answered.

I had driven just a few blocks, when she asked, *"Would you mind driving a little faster, just for today?"* She laughed, then added, *"I'd like to get there before dark."*

I'd never seen Barbara so excited. She talked nonstop about the gift she'd made for her mother without telling me what it was. She was certain her mother would love it. As she talked, I remembered a time when I was a seven-year-old in art class. I glued a piece of burlap cloth on a board and then painted a picture of an Indian pottery jar on it. After the paint dried, I glued tiny sequins all over the jar, then outlined it with yarn. I even painted a desert in the background. I worked diligently to make it beautiful. It was a gift for my mother. To me, it was the most beautiful picture in the whole world. I couldn't wait for school to be out that day. All I could think about was the gift in my desk. That afternoon, the school bus seemed to go slower than ever and I was certain I'd never make it home before dark. At long last, the bus door swung open and out I jumped. I couldn't believe my eyes! The hill I climbed every day to get home had most certainly grown higher and steeper while I'd been at school—all because of a painting tucked safely under my arm.

I looked over at Barbara and saw a little girl in a grown-up body, eager to present a priceless gift to her mother and I drove just a little faster.

We arrived at the nursing home, (before dark, to Barbara's delight) and Barbara got settled in her wheelchair. We began our usual 'take your time and enjoy the journey' routine. Nevertheless, it was just a matter of minutes before Barbara patted my hand and said, *"Do you think we could go a little faster, dear? I'm really anxious to see my mother."*

I laughed and answered, *"Sure. Hold onto your britches."*

Her wheelchair became my motorcycle. I twisted the handlebars, revved up the engine and off we went for a wild ride. We flew past Sister Jane, slowing down just long enough for Barbara to invite her to join us in a race. Sister Jane laughed and politely declined. We took off again and Barbara clutched her purse as we rounded the corner, then swung to the left barely missing a laundry rack. Laughing hilariously, we made it to her mother's room in record time and in one piece. I parked Barbara under the window beside her mother's chair, then quickly stepped back to watch. I had a feeling this was going to be a moment I'd never forget.

Wasting no time, Barbara reached in her purse and brought out a rather small piece of neatly folded, white tissue paper. A delicate, yellow ribbon was wrapped around it and tied in a miniature bow. Such a simple package, yet, obviously so valuable.

Lovingly, she handed the gift to her mother and said, *"I've something of yours that once was broken and scattered. It was lost forever, or so you thought. I collected the pieces, put them back together and made something beautiful from them. Just for you, Mom. Just because I love you."*

Her mother reached out and with trembling hands opened her gift. Inside the paper, were the scattered beads made into a brand new, beautiful necklace. Barbara had painstakingly re-strung the beads and the result was a necklace even prettier than before. Helen's eyes filled with tears, as she repeatedly hugged and thanked her daughter.

Barbara placed the necklace around her mother's neck. It was quite long and came to rest right over her heart. How appropriate, I thought.

In writing this story, I find myself thinking about how God does the same thing for us. He takes the broken, scattered, impossible events of our lives, things that we think are lost forever and He makes them beautiful. Broken lives become masterpieces with just a touch of the Master's hand, and why? Just because He loves us.

"He's made *all* things beautiful in its time." Ecclesiastes 3:11

Barbara and I left Helen's room that day filled with incredible joy.

Barbara continued to visit not only her mother, but also others, in spite of the many challenges the cancer created for her. She had a strong desire to help those who were suffering. And so it was, that she asked me if I knew anyone who was sick and in need of a friend. At that time I didn't, then just a few days later, I met Lisa, a young mother who'd just been diagnosed with liver cancer. Two days later, Barbara went with me to visit her. From that time on, she and her husband, Phil made many visits to this family. When Lisa became too sick to attend church services, they brought church to her. We joined them as they prayed, read scriptures and sang with Lisa, as she lay on the couch, too weak to sit up. Barbara and Phil continued to encourage and love Lisa and her family to the end.

All the while, Barbara continued to push back her own pain and keep going. She amazed me with the way she consistently put the needs of others ahead of her own. Barbara certainly knew what true riches were and, I'm sure, had many treasures awaiting her arrival in heaven. Was serving others easy for her? No, but she'd certainly tell you it was worth it. Was sacrificial love convenient for her? No, never. She had to go through ten times the preparations we do just to be able to leave her house. Barbara couldn't drive a car nor walk very far. Her pain was constant. Was life hard for Barbara? If you had asked her that question, I don't believe she would've said that it was. I learned from her that life isn't really hard when *others* are your focus. I believe I can tell you what would've been hard for Barbara—doing nothing and blessing no one, that would've made her life unbearable.

Throughout that last year, Barbara's spirit grew stronger, though not her body. The tumor was silently, secretly destroying her liver. She sensed something was really wrong a couple of months before her doctors discovered it. One morning she said, *"Rhonda, would you pray for me? This time, I don't think I'll make it. I still have so much fear and I need prayer for the Lord to give me His peace. You know, like Psalm 23...'When I walk through the valley of the shadow of death, I will fear no evil. For Thou art with me.' Well, that's exactly what I need."*

My heart sank at this news. Somehow, I managed to pray without breaking down. Nonetheless, as soon as I drove away, the river of tears flowed. My heart cried out for the Lord to heal her, as I knew He could.

Over the next several weeks, we spent time praying for the peace she longed for and asking the Lord to heal her body. I watched as this brave soul worked through her fears and finally found the peace she'd been crying out for.

Two weeks later, in January, she was hospitalized and the hidden tumor was discovered. She was told she had just a few weeks left and was sent home. Meals were brought in and a long list of friends volunteered to sit with Barbara. She was too sick to leave her house, so we brought church to her—just as she'd done so many times for others.

The Sunday before Barbara went to be with Jesus, a group of us were singing hymns while she sat in her recliner. She looked so beautiful. Her eyes were closed and her lips moved ever so gently, as she worshipped her Maker. The light from a nearby lamp cast a golden glow on her face, as if a heavenly light was resting on her, in preparation for her soon journey home. Her hands were folded in her lap. I closed my eyes, unable to bear anymore. After some time, I looked back at Barbara and tears were streaming down her sweet face. I quietly went and knelt beside her. I took her petite, little hand in mine and gently caressed it. Her skin was baby soft, incredibly young looking and absolutely flawless. I'd always admired Barbara's beautiful hands. They were so gentle, kind and loving. I wondered just how many people her hands had blessed during her lifetime; I was certain it was many.

I looked into her incredible, crystal blue eyes that were so full of tears and asked if she was in pain. She whispered, *"My physical pain is nothing compared to the pain I have in my heart. My heart's hurting because I've been so angry with the Lord today. I've been questioning His will for my life and I don't want to be found doubting Him ever again. He's God and I'm not, so guess who should yield? You know, sometimes God says no and that answer hurts."*

What an incredible heart this woman of God had! We joined hands and prayed. She confessed her sin, asked God to forgive her and to give her the grace to make it to the finish line with a pure heart. I began to softly sing, 'It Is Well With My Soul'. A sweet peace replaced our tears.

"All is well," she whispered.

We talked. Barbara told me that she felt Jesus would be coming for her very soon. I knew in my heart that she was right. We held each other for a long time and cried. I thanked the Lord for this dear friend He'd blessed me with and for the time I had with her.

The following day began a dramatic decline in Barbara's physical condition, even though, her spirit soared as she fixed her eyes upon her destination. Each day that week, her mother sat by her bed holding her hand. Many times they'd just sit in silence, allowing their tears to say what they had no words for. Day after day,

Helen told Barbara not to leave her, that she needed her. Barbara reassured her mother that she wasn't leaving just yet.

On Wednesday, Helen noticed Barbara's forehead was drawn tight, a manifestation of the pain that racked her body. Helen asked me, *"Is she in pain?"*

I nodded. Helen looked at her daughter lying there and said, *"Barb, I don't know how I'll make it without you. You've been such a good daughter and have taken such good care of me. If you go, who will take care of me?"*

Barbara squeezed her mother's hand and weakly answered, *"Mom, just hold onto Jesus' hand just like you're holding onto mine. He'll take good care of you."*

No one understood that more than Barbara.

Helen then wiped the tears from her daughter's face and said, *"Barb, if you need to go and be with Jesus, it's okay with me. Don't worry about me."*

Barbara replied, *"Okay, mom."*

The love Barbara had so freely given through the years was now being lavished upon her as a steady stream of friends expressed their love for her over the next two days. Barbara loved much; therefore she was much loved.

The day before she died, Lee Harms, a pastor and friend, came to see her. He talked with her, then prayed for Barbara and her husband. Just before Lee left, he turned to Barbara, took her hand and asked if there was anything else he could do for her.

She nodded. She was very weak and it required a great deal of effort, but finally she managed to whisper, *"Remember to pray for my husband."*

He assured her that he would. We looked at each other and tears instantly filled our eyes. Even now, when the pain was unbearable, she was thinking of others. Lee left and I stood holding her hand. I looked down at my dear friend. With tears flowing like a river down my face and onto her sheets, I whispered, *"Barbara, you look so much like Jesus to me."*

The next day, Barbara slipped into a deep sleep. She couldn't open her eyes, nor talk. I stayed by her side as much as possible, not wanting to leave my friend. I reassured her that all was well and everything was taken care of. I reminded her that I'd see her mother was well cared for. Silent tears fell from her closed eyes. I wiped her tears and mine, as I sang to her for the last time, 'It Is Well With My Soul'. Then, kissing her forehead, I said good-bye to my dear friend.

That night, all of her family encircled her bed and for over an hour sang beautiful hymns to a beautiful Lord. Barbara listened and waited. Shortly after nine p.m. they sang, 'Turn Your Eyes Upon Jesus', and just as they sang, '...look full in His lovely face', Barbara instantly opened her eyes. Suddenly, her eyes filled with tears as she looked across the room, focusing on an unseen visitor. A tangible Presence filled the room and covered everyone like a warm blanket. Her face instantly reflected His glory and she left this life with her one true Love.

* * * * * * * * *

Two years later, Barbara's mother still wears her beautiful necklace. It is by far, her favorite. She shows it off every chance she gets and tells everyone who will listen about her wonderful daughter, Barbara. Helen continues to hold tightly to Jesus' hand. He's taking extra good care of her, just like Barbara said He would.

In honor of my dear friend, Barbara.

PORTRAIT OF A LOVELY LADY

She walks in love. Her touch is soft and so are her ways. Her eyes are alive with the love of her Father. Her heart beats with compassion and tenderness. Hands created to serve. Faithful friend. Listening heart. Sacrifice is her middle name. Her words are life, no death found here. Abounding in grace, ever mindful of others. Speaking praise and extremely hesitant to find fault.

Her Shepherd ordains her steps and she willingly follows. Her heart grows in confidence, not in herself, but in her Maker and Keeper. Faith, hope and love are her portion. She is a deep well. Never wavering. Never doubting. Rejoicing as she runs with Him over the mountaintop. Ever submitting to her Master's hand as He leads her through deep valleys.

A tree firmly planted by the water. A silent sufferer, no complaining leaves her lips. She is strong in her commitment to the truth, yet ever so gentle. Laughter in the midst of sorrow. Peace in the throes of the hurricane. Never despairing. Never quitting. Not understanding, yet always trusting. Keeping the cross ever before her face. Living and loving the good news. Faithful and obedient unto death.

She cries out, *"Where is my Beloved?"*

She looks! She searches! She waits for Him. The journey has been good. The journey has been hard. She longs for wings that she might fly away. Her heart leaps within—for on the horizon, she strains to see... *"Could it be the One I've waited for? The One I've sought after?"*

Her eyes behold Him. In all His glory, she sees Him! Oh, the beauty of this Son of Man! The Love of her life! Perfection manifested before her. The day she's waited for has come at last! She calls out, *"Come for me, My Lord."*

He comes to her. Arms of love surround her. He whispers to her waiting heart, *"I've waited so long for this day."*

Slowly, she looks up into the face of her King. Oh, what love she sees! The Lamb of God! She exclaims, *"My Savior, my Redeemer, my Friend!"*

She clings to Him and refuses to let Him go. Joy floods her soul. All that she's suffered is quickly forgotten. She thinks only of Him. Rivers of peace wash over her. Grace and glory cover her. Warmth fills her soul. Then, she looks down. Grief fills her for her garments are but filthy rags. Her head drops in shame and she steps back. Immediately, her Savior steps toward her and lifts her face; He smiles. Oh, a thousand smiles could never equal one of His!

She whispers, *"This love I feel, how can this be? How can You look upon me with such tenderness, for I am wretched and dressed in filthy rags?"*

He answers, *"You are altogether beautiful, My sister, My bride. For I've washed you in My blood and made you lovely. Look again, for you are pure and spotless and there is no blemish in you."*

She looks. Her rags have been replaced with a garment of the finest linen, dazzling in appearance, pure white. No spot, nor wrinkle. No blemish. Complete perfection.

He takes her hand in His and says, *"Now is the time. Rise up, My fair one, My perfect one and come away with Me."*

His nail-scarred hands wipe away her tears. Sweet, sweet release. All is well. Love is fulfilled. Looking full into His face, she says, *"I am Yours and You are mine—for all of eternity."*

Eternity opens its doors. No more sorrow. No more pain. He leads her on. Jesus—the reason she lived, now becomes her reason for dying.

The music plays and the dance begins. . . .

CHAPTER EIGHTEEN

Grandma

And Jesus answered and said,
"You shall love the Lord your God with all your heart,
and with all your soul,
And with all your strength, and with all your mind;
And your neighbor as yourself."
Luke 10:27

One neighbor helping another—it's as simple as that.

There's a widow who lives on the street behind our house. She has a name, but few people know what it is. Everyone, whether old or young, just call her, 'Grandma.'

I first heard about Grandma at Kid's Explosion, which is our neighborhood children's outreach that meets weekly in a park near Grandma's house.

After hearing several of the children talk about Grandma, I asked one of the girls who this Grandma was that they talked so much about. She couldn't believe I didn't know her; after all, everybody knows Grandma! The word spread quickly and soon I had ten excited children telling me about this lady. They said she wasn't really their grandma, yet acts like one just the same. She does everything a real Grandma does: feeds them, tells them stories, and grows the most beautiful flowers in the whole neighbor-hood.

When I heard about the flowers, I immediately knew which house was Grandma's. There was only one house in this neighbor-hood which fit that description. For several years, I had admired her beautiful flowers and on many occasions, had slowed down to a turtle's pace just to admire the beauty of a multitude of tulips in full bloom.

I knew I had to meet Grandma.

After Kid's Explosion, two of the children, Chandal and Lance were going to Grandma's, so I asked if I could tag along. Chandal said Grandma would feed us lunch. On the way there, she told me 'Grandma stories'. I was learning why all the children loved her so.

On the corner was Grandma's house, just as full of color as ever. Patches of fire blazed before us as vibrant tulips of every color swayed in the breeze. Everywhere I looked, on every corner, in the middle and along both sides of her yard stood a multitude of these noble flowers.

Tulips have always been one of my favorite flowers. I tried to stop and admire their magnificent beauty, but Chandal and Lance were hungry so they pulled me across the yard to the front door. Without knocking, they walked through her unlocked door and into the living room.

In unison they said, *"Hi, Grandma. We brought somebody to meet you."*

Grandma got up from her couch and warmly welcomed me. I told her I'd heard good things about her from the neighborhood children. She blushed and quickly turned her attention to the chil-dren, asking if they were hungry. They looked at me and grinned, their eyes said, "I told you so." They told Grandma they were more than hungry, they were starving. She laughed and invited me to join her in the kitchen.

We stepped into a room that was quite small. In every possible nook and cranny, beautiful houseplants grew, filling the kitchen with life and color. The once white walls were yellowed. The appliances looked old enough to be the original ones installed when the house was built many years before. The floor was covered with linoleum that was very faded and ripped in many places. As I walked across the kitchen, the floor sank under my feet. I carefully stepped closer to the door.

Grandma sat down at a small metal table and opened a jar of peanut butter. I looked closer at this woman as she spread love on pieces of bread. Her thin, grayish-white hair was pulled up in a bun on the top of her head. A few wisps of hair had escaped the bobby pins and hung in spirals on her neck. She had a kind face and her soft wrinkles only added to that gentleness. A faint rose color adorned her cheeks. Her clear, blue eyes danced happily as she talked about the neighborhood children. She wore a pale, pink sweatshirt and sweatpants. Hand painted on the front of her shirt were the words, 'Grandma's are the best'. I told her I loved her shirt and she said, *"This shirt's very special because one of the children down the street made it as a gift for me."*

I followed as she carried more than a dozen sandwiches to the table. She called Chandal and Lance to the table. They helped themselves and then Grandma handed me a sandwich. I sank my teeth into the delicious peanut butter and jelly sandwich. As I chewed, I wondered why food made by Grandma's tastes so good.

I looked at the plate and it was still full. I asked Grandma why she made so many sandwiches. Chuckling, she answered, *"You'll see."*

I'd almost finished eating when the door opened and three more children came inside. She offered them a sandwich and they eagerly accepted.

She looked at me and smiled, *"That's why."*

It was only a matter of minutes before several more neighborhood children dropped in for lunch and Grandma hurriedly made more sandwiches.

After a very pleasant visit, I thanked Grandma for her hospitality. She invited me to come back anytime. Stepping onto the street, I turned to admire Grandma's yard once more. The flowers waved a friendly farewell, providing a wonderful frame for Grandma standing in her doorway, smiling. I waved goodbye then looked at the fiery-red tulips near my feet. Bending over to touch their little heads, I said, *"Little tulips, you sure make this house beautiful; I've been quite taken by your loveliness today."*

I began making regular trips to Grandma's house. Through the years, I've learned a lot about this quiet servant. I discovered that Grandma was 68-years-old, her husband died many years ago, she doesn't own a car and never goes anywhere. She can't even remember the last time she bought clothes for herself. She loves cats almost as much as children and she absolutely adores Velveeta cheese. She has a granddaughter in college named Rhonda and a grandson who uses her bedroom walls as a canvas, covering them with wonderful paintings and sketches. Her monthly income was approximately three hundred dollars, which meant she had no heat in the winter and no air conditioning in the summer. Her bed was a thirty year old sofa. She lived in a house that was in need of repair, but was quite content with her life because she believes things aren't so important—people are. And last, but certainly not least, I learned that she's a faithful follower of Jesus.

I also learned that this is one busy lady. Two years ago, Grandma earned the Citizens of the Year award because of her service to the community. Not only does she lovingly care for the neighborhood children, but she also takes care of the park, picking up broken glass and trash. Grandma is the reason the park has several flowerbeds filled with gorgeous tulips. Over the years, she's planted several trees along the highway in front of her house. On a regular basis, she checks on her elderly neighbor, taking her food and doing whatever needs to be done.

One day last summer, I saw her mowing the lawn of a house several doors up from hers. I put my car in reverse. Sweat was running down Grandma's face and her shirt was soaked. Leaning out my window, I asked why she was mowing this yard.

She said, *"The lady who lives here needs help. I have a mower, she doesn't. I have the time, she doesn't. One neighbor helping another neighbor, it's as simple as that. Somebody needed to help her and today, that somebody's me."*

That's Grandma for you.

Three years ago, Grandma heard about a single mother in her neighborhood that had been offered a job at the post office. This mother had been unable to find affordable child-care for her two-month-old. Without hesitation, Grandma offered to take care of her baby while she worked. When the subject of pay came up, Grandma refused to accept any. When I asked why she'd do that, she responded, *"The way I figure it, she had a need and I had the means to meet that need. I figure it must be very difficult raising a child alone, so if I'm in a position to care for her child, why should I be paid for that? It doesn't cost me anything and it's so good for me to have a little one around, it keeps me young. Besides, it's about one neighbor helping another."*

To this day, she still cares for this little girl. And she does so without pay—here on earth, that is.

A couple of months ago we learned that her property was going to be auctioned because she'd been unable to pay her taxes. Danny asked her what she was going to do. She said, *"There's nothing I can do. I don't have any way to come up with the money. Regardless, I learned along time ago not to worry about things I can't do anything about, that only makes one miserable."*

Three weeks later, our ministry was able to pay her taxes. We gave her a card that said: "Remember, one neighbor helping another neighbor. It's as simple as that."

Today, as I drove by Grandma's house, I slowed down for the hundredth time to admire her vibrant yard. The sun was shining clear and bright, the birds were singing songs of spring and the air was filled with a sweet fragrance. Once again, her armies of tulips were in full bloom. They held their heads high, proud of the brilliant colors that adorned them. Kneeling in the midst of them was Grandma. She had a spade in one hand and her other hand rested on the handle of a large wicker basket. What a beautiful picture!

I stopped my car. She looked up at me and smiled. Her precious, little face was smudged with dirt. The wind had set a good portion of her hair free from its nest and it blew gracefully in the breeze. I waved at this lovely lady. Her whole face lit up. She waved back with her spade. If only I had had a camera.

I continued on towards my destination. A warm feeling swept over me as I thought of Grandma. While stopped at a red light, I looked up into the great expanse before me. The white, fluffy clouds were racing to an unknown destination. I said, *"Lord, You certainly created this earth and all it contains to be breathtakingly beautiful. But you know, Lord, even surrounded by this incredible beauty, I believe Grandma is the most beautiful of them all."*

* * * * * * * * *

The multitude of gorgeous tulips I once thought were the crowning beauty of Grandma's house, I now saw as a mere reflection of the one who planted them. And, the one who planted them as a mere reflection of Jesus.

Over five years have gone by since I first met Grandma. She's clearly demonstrated, many times over, that loving your neighbor means looking for opportunities to serve, which often requires some form of sacrifice.

But it's definitely worth it. And it really is that simple.

Grandma standing among her beautiful tulips.

CHAPTER NINETEEN

No Greater Love

This is My commandment, that you love one another,
just as I have loved you.
Greater love has no one than this that one
lay down his life for his friends.
John 14:12-13

Courage is not the absence of fear.
Courage is taking action in the midst of fear.

𝕿here's no way I could write this book without sharing the following story. A story of one of the bravest, most selfless acts I've experienced. It still moves me to this day.

It was early March and the homeless team was wrapping up another evening of ministry. As was our custom, we joined hands with the remaining homeless people and formed a circle to pray. David, a homeless man, and Mocky were standing directly across from me. There were about twenty people in the circle, a little more than half were our homeless friends. We took turns praying. This was one of my favorite parts of the evening. I loved to hear the homeless pray because their words flow out of a lifestyle that's totally dependent on God, in ways I've never experienced.

David was praying, when suddenly there was quite a commotion behind us. I looked up to see a man running as fast as his legs would carry him in our direction. Behind him was a police officer in hot pursuit. The policeman had his hand on his gun and was yelling for the man to stop. He kept running. From the street behind raced two police cars with their spotlights searching the darkness trying to lock their beams on the fleeing man.

David shouted for us to get down as he plunged face first in the dirt. Everyone, except our team, immediately dropped to the ground. It was clear who was from the suburbs and who wasn't—we were the ones standing with our mouths open and our eyes wide.

It never occurred to me that we might be in danger. David crawled over to us and with great intensity, said it would be a good idea for us to get down on the ground. But, everything was happening so fast; we just stood there. The fleeing man continued to run directly toward us. Suddenly, Mocky stepped out from behind me and stood in front of me. I didn't want to miss anything so I stepped out from behind her. She stepped back in front of me. I wondered what she was doing. I stepped aside again and so did she. That was when I realized she was trying to protect me. I tested my theory and she once more stepped between the fleeing man and me. I was so stunned, I forgot about the drama happening in front of us. Without warning, the fleeing man pushed his way through the middle of our little group with the policeman just a few feet behind him. Mocky remained in front of me with her arms outstretched, shielding me with her body! She stayed in that position even when the policeman ran past and one of the police cars jumped the curb and raced through Jurassic Park. Only after they disappeared into the darkness, did she relax her protective stance.

My circuits were overloaded; I wandered around like a lost puppy while everyone else loaded the van. As we drove home, the van was alive with excitement. Each person talked about the wild event, everyone that is, except Mocky and me. We sat in silence. I finally leaned over and whispered a thank you to Mocky. She smiled and nodded. We rode the rest of the way in silence.

I had trouble falling asleep that night, so I quietly slipped out of bed, put on my coat and house shoes, and went outside on our deck. The bitter cold threatened to chase me back inside, so I pulled my coat even closer around me. It was a good, secure feeling.

I looked up at the crisp, night sky. My body began to relax as I drank in its splendor. As long as I can remember, I've been fascinated with the heavens. I've longed to see the Creator hidden behind the dark canvas and see the splendor of heaven. On this clear night I found myself being drawn to the beauty of the night sky; the full moon was shining with all its strength. The stars seemed to be clapping their hands and dancing in adoration of the King of all kings. The North Star clearly pointed heavenward. The beauty of it all carried me back to a night when I was a child. A night when the stars were just as bright and the moon just as brilliant. Back to an evening, when my eight-year-old imagination soared heavenward. I pictured God standing before a full-length mirror in His Throne Room. His glory blinded me! I had to look away. A multitude of angels filled the place; they all bowed before the King. Suddenly, God turned His gaze from the mirror and looked out into time and space. He saw that the heavens were void of light. This would never do. How would the man He was about to create ever comprehend His glory and the light of His presence, if they lived in a world of complete darkness? God spoke and the mirror before Him exploded into millions of various sized pieces. In that moment, God's awesome beauty was embedded into the pieces of glass. The fragments then hurled through space coming to rest at their God-ordained place in the heavens. The darkness now knew light. And so would mankind.

Taking a deep breath, I turned my attention back to the heavens and softly sang love songs to my Savior. It seemed that all of nature joined in my worship—the rustling of the trees, the ebb and flow of the wind, and the fast running stream. A shooting star streaked across the sky underlining the magnificence of it all. What beauty! All was well.

"Dearest Father, I keep thinking about what Mocky did for me tonight. She was willing to risk being hurt in order to protect me. This is the same Mocky who used to be so afraid of people she couldn't even talk to them. It's amazing how much she's changed and all because of You. You are indeed good to us."

* * * * * * * * * *

You Saw My Sin

Before I came into this world,
You saw my sin and stood between it and me.
With no regard to Your own comfort
And knowing the price You would pay,
With my life ever before Your loving eyes,
You stood firm in Your devotion to me.

With Your arms stretched out
And a heart beating to the Song of all Songs,
You took the penalty for all my sins
And shielded me from eternal death.
Oh, my Lord and King, I'm ever so grateful
And I thank You for loving and saving me.

—Rhonda

CHAPTER TWENTY

Blind Faith

That though He was rich, yet for your sake He became poor,
That you through His poverty might become rich.
II Corinthians 8:9

True poverty isn't about money or the lack thereof.
True poverty is a life lived without Jesus.

At Kid's Explosion, I met one of the richest people I've ever known. Her name is Anita.

It was the first day of our third location for Kid's Explosion in Kansas City. One of my 'jobs' was to make name badges for the children. That's when I met nine-year-old Misty. My oldest daughter's name is Misty, so I was immediately drawn to this little one.

In the weeks that passed, I talked to Misty every chance I had. Each time, she'd just smile and shyly look away. It was nearly a month before she would respond with more than two words. She remained very timid and quite fearful, but there was a sweetness about her that was endearing.

A couple of months into our program, Misty stayed to help me pack the Kid's Explosion supplies. So, I took advantage of the opportunity and asked if I could walk her home and meet her mother. She said, *"I live with my grandma."*

I replied, *"Okay, I'd love to meet your grandmother then."*

She knocked on her grandmother's door; her cousin unlocked the dead bolt. As we walked in, Misty announced, *"Hi, Grandma, I brought someone to meet you."*

Her grandmother, Anita, greeted me warmly. She said that Misty loved Kid's Explosion and talked about it all the time. Bouncing around, Misty interrupted. She was eager to tell Anita what she had learned that morning. While Misty told her grandmother about Daniel and the lions, I looked around the room. I couldn't believe what I was seeing! Anita was sitting on the only piece of furniture in the room and it was a lawn chair. Misty's cousin was sitting on the floor playing with the cat. I looked through the door into the kitchen; the room was absolutely empty. Even the counter tops were bare. I tried to be inconspicuous as I looked down the hall into the open door of a bedroom. All I could see was a pillow and a sheet neatly folded in the corner. I turned my attention back to Misty and her grandmother. Anita was listening intently with her hands folded in her lap. Suddenly, I realized Anita was blind. I was overwhelmed with emotion. Tears welled up in my eyes and I decided it would be best for me to leave. I asked if I could stop by for a visit later in the week, then said good-bye. I literally ran to the van. With tears flowing down my face, I told my husband what I'd just seen.

A few days later, Danny and I went for a visit. What I suspected was true; there were no beds or furniture in the house. Anita slept on the floor, along with her three grandchildren. I learned they had recently fled an abusive situation and had to leave everything behind. They came to Kansas City with very little money, yet she was so happy to be in a safe place that none of that mattered.

In spite of all the difficult things she'd endured throughout her long life, Anita was a delight. Danny and I thoroughly enjoyed our visit with Anita and she invited us to come back anytime. As we drove away, we asked the Lord to provide a bed for Anita.

The very next day a lady from our church called and said she had a twin bed she wanted to give away. She asked if I knew anyone who needed one. Did I ever! That same afternoon Danny loaded the bed on his truck and we headed straight for Anita's apartment. Anita was surprised to see us back so soon. I told her we had asked the Lord to provide a bed for her and He had answered right away. She somewhat hesitantly said, *"I really appreciate the bed and I don't want you to think I don't. But I was wondering if I could give it to Misty? As for me, I don't mind the floor, but it really bothers me that my three grandchildren are sleeping on the floor."*

I immediately sent up a prayer for three more beds realizing Anita was going to see that her grandchildren had beds before she accepted one.

In just a couple of weeks, God provided two beds, two dressers, two night tables, a couch, three living room chairs, a coffee table, end tables, kitchen utensils, a kitchen table and four chairs, lamps, and numerous pictures to brighten up the walls. When we brought the pictures in I wondered if Anita would want them. When I asked her, she responded, *"Oh, yes, I'd love to have them. Even if I can't see them, my grandchildren can."*

She asked me to describe every picture in detail. Before we left that day, her fifteen-year-old granddaughter had already begun hanging them.

Finally, Anita's apartment was fully furnished and looked nice. I told her we were still asking the Lord for a bed for her now that all her grandchildren had one. She answered, *"Oh, please don't bother. I couldn't use it if you gave me one. I only have two bedrooms and it's important to me that my grandchildren have their own rooms. I have a couch and that's all I need."*

I left realizing I'd been asking the Lord for the wrong thing. Anita didn't need a bed. What she needed was a comfortable sleeper sofa. The sofa she had wasn't the most comfortable thing to sit on, so I knew it must be even worse to sleep on. You may find this hard to believe but just three days later, I received a phone call from someone who said, *"I just bought a new sofa and was wondering if you knew anyone who could use my old sleeper sofa. It's in great shape. I'd like it to go to someone who really needs it."*

The following day, Anita's face beamed as she continually ran her hand over the fabric of her very comfortable sleeper sofa.

The first week of December, a Christmas tree and all the trimmings were donated. You guessed it; we took them to Anita and her grandchildren. We spent the evening with them eating popcorn, drinking hot chocolate and talking about the true meaning of Christmas. It was great.

One day, I asked Anita how she became blind. She said, *"Many years ago, when I was in my early twenties, I was struck by a hit-and-run driver as I crossed the street. The accident broke every bone on the left side of my body and catapulted me into pitch-blackness, leaving me permanently blind. After three months in the hospital, I went home in a wheelchair to five very young children, one less than a year old. My doctors told me I'd spend the rest of my life in that chair. My husband decided he didn't want a blind, crippled wife so he left. I never heard from him again.*

I spent the next five months just sitting in my wheelchair, in the dark. That's all I did. One day, I decided I'd sat there long enough; I was going to get out of that chair and take care of my children. I asked a friend to buy me a pair of crutches and I began the hard work of learning how to walk again. Within a couple of months, I was able to walk short distances with my crutches. Several months later, I was taking steps unaided. I soon gave my crutches away.

I raised all five of my children alone. About three years ago, me and my fourteen-year-old granddaughter moved to Kansas City to get away from a real bad situation and to be near my daughter and her children. It wasn't long before Misty moved in with me because her mother has to be at work before Misty leaves for school. Within two months, my grandson from Oklahoma moved in."

As I listened, all I could think about was what an incredible woman this was so I told her so. She responded, *"No, I'm not. I just needed to be able to care for my children. I had to walk because my children needed me. If it wasn't for my children, I'm certain I'd still be in that wheelchair today. And, as for my grandchildren, well they need me, too."*

Anita hesitated, then said, *"Can I ask you a question?"*

"Of course."

"Could my grandchildren and I go to church with you Sunday?"

This was the moment we'd been praying for! The following Sunday, Anita and her three grandchildren attended church with us.

A few weeks later, a couple from church heard about Anita's situation and offered to 'adopt' the family. Frank and Pam began to reach out to them with love and friendship.

Then, one Sunday morning, Pam led Anita in prayer as she gave her life to Jesus. And soon thereafter, her daughter and three grandchildren followed in her footsteps.

I so admire Anita. She gets up at 4:00 a.m. Monday through Friday to iron her grandchildren's clothes, cook breakfast, and get them off for school. Anita's income is less than $350 per month. That's all she has to buy food, pay her utilities and rent (she lives in subsidized housing).

On one of my visits to Anita's, a couple from Norway went with me. Their hearts were so touched by her situation that they gave me some money to buy Anita some new clothes. I called Anita, told her the good news and set a date to take her shopping.

The day arrived and Anita timidly told me she needed food more than clothing. She asked if it would be okay if we went to the grocery store instead. Needless to say, we went to the grocery store. Once in the store, I told her to buy whatever she wanted. She turned to her two granddaughters, Misty and Robbie and told them to pick out whatever they wanted. I watched, as this ten and fifteen-year-old made their selections: shampoo, soap, toothpaste, deodorant, fresh fruit, fresh vegetables, macaroni and cheese, spaghetti sauce and noodles, rice, cookies, juice, various meats, cereal, coffee (for Grandma), cheese, milk, peanut butter, jelly, various canned vegetables, and paper goods. Twice they quit shopping, but I encouraged them to buy more. Having filled their cart, they made their way to the checkout talking in low whispers about all the 'extras' they got.

I was filled with a mixture of sadness and joy. Sadness because the things most of us consider necessities, they considered 'extra' and joy because they were so thrilled. After we unloaded the groceries in their apartment, Anita laid her hand on my arm and thanked me. I looked in the kitchen and saw Misty and Robbie laughing and talking non-stop as they put the food away. That was good enough for me.

On another occasion, a dreary, cold February day, I picked Anita up for our monthly trip to the grocery store. I was very tired, so I was rather quiet. It actually was a good thing because Anita ended up doing most of the talking. She talked about the poverty she'd lived in all of her life. She described the rats she had to chase away from her babies and the fear she lived with because of the violence that was so prevalent in her poverty-stricken neighborhood. She talked of the various difficulties she encountered raising her children as a single mother.

As I pulled into the parking space, Anita ended her story with this statement, *"when I was poor, it was very hard for me."*

I was stunned! Perhaps I'd heard her wrong so I asked, *"Anita, did you say, 'When I was poor?'"*

She answered, *"Yeah. When I was poor, it was very hard."*

Still in shock I said, *"Anita, you are supporting yourself and three grandchildren on less than $350 per month. That's less than most people bring home in a week. What do you mean, 'when you were poor?'"*

She said, *"That's exactly what I mean. I use to be poor and now I'm not. Before I knew Jesus, I was poor. I spent over sixty years in that kind of poverty and I don't ever want go back. That's true poverty. Now, when something goes wrong or I need something, I have someone to turn to—Jesus and He helps me. I can't see Him because I'm blind, but I know He's right here beside me all the time. He may not always give me exactly what I want, and that's okay cause He knows best. No, I'm definitely not poor anymore."*

She was right. I was wrong. Anita is one of the richest people I know!

* * * * * * * * *

Anita continues to follow the Lord. Just three months ago, she moved from her apartment into a house with her daughter. Her neighborhood had grown steadily worse to the point that Anita was concerned for the safety of her grandchildren.

Things are still financially difficult for Anita. But, she continues to grow richer, day by day.

Part V

AN INNER CITY NEIGHBORHOOD

And let us not lose heart in doing good,
For in due time we shall reap
if we don't grow weary.
Galatians 6:9

THE HARVEST FIELD

Dry, dusty land.
Rocks, thorns and thistles.
Hot, burning sun,
Clouds that give no water.

The laborers are few
And refreshment is scarce.
The work is hard
But the pay is like no other.

The fields are ready
For plowing, sowing and harvesting.
Pray to the Master
To send laborers into the forgotten fields.
—Rhonda

CHAPTER TWENTY-ONE

The Building

"For I know the plans that I have for you,"
declares the Lord, "Plans for welfare and not
for calamity to give you a future and a hope."
Jeremiah 29:11

Never be afraid to trust an unknown future to a known God.
He knows the way.

$\mathfrak{I}$t was Sunday, Danny and I were getting ready to leave church when a friend came running up and said, *"That young man over there asked if I knew anyone who ministers in the inner city. I told him about you. He'd like to talk with you, if you have the time."*

We didn't realize that our lives were about to change dramatically. After we introduced ourselves to Andrew, he got right to the point, *"My father's a pastor and owns a building in the inner city. He's looking for a ministry that would like to use his building to reach out into the community in exchange for making some necessary repairs. Would you be interested?"*

At that time, we weren't looking for a building and had absolutely no experience working in the inner city. We'd been feeding the homeless, but that hardly qualified us to take on such an enormous task. We exchanged phone numbers and told Andrew we'd definitely pray about it.

Within an hour of arriving home, Andrew's father called and invited us to see the building. We made an appointment in two weeks. That gave us time to pray.

Danny and I grew up in the country. I asked myself why I would even consider working in an inner city neighborhood. I was definitely not qualified for something like this. I thought that settled it and I had my answer. That night, I had a dream where I sat at a table. A prophet handed me a folder filled with a record of my entire life. I read the report then laid it aside. The man then handed me another folder and asked me to deliver the message inside it to a particular group of people. I was filled with fear and uncertainty. *"I can't; I'm not qualified. I can't speak well enough."* I said. I thought of Moses and his inability to speak, I continued, *"I need Aaron. Where's Aaron?"* The man then turned to someone else, handed him the folder and then asked if he'd go. Without any hesitation, that man agreed. My heart was instantly sad; I knew I'd just missed an opportunity to serve God. I'd allowed my fears and insecurities to overcome my trust in God's ability to help me. When I awoke, I immediately thought of the invitation we'd been given to take the gospel into the inner city and I knew we had to accept this offer.

The day before our appointment to see the building, the pastor called, *"I want to let you know things have changed since we talked. I believe the Lord told me I'm supposed to give you the building instead of allowing you to use it. So, if you want it, it's yours."*

Needless to say, Danny and I were very shocked. As we drove into the city, I told myself the building must be dilapidated and in need of a good bulldozer. But, it wasn't that way at all. The building definitely needed repairs, but, over all, it was sound and usable just as it was.

The moment I stepped inside, I knew I was in the right place.

* * * * * * * * *

Just one month later, we were the new owners of a building in one of Kansas City's highest crime rate areas—and we were thrilled. We found ourselves, suddenly, thrust on a path of insecurity and inadequacy, where one learns to trust God at a new level.

Our journey was just beginning....

CHAPTER TWENTY-TWO

Just Like Family

*You prepare a table before me in the presence of my enemies;
You have anointed my head with oil; my cup overflows.
Surely goodness and lovingkindness will follow me
all the days of my life, and I will dwell in the
House of the Lord forever.*
Psalm 23:5-6

There is a Love that knows no boundaries,
no race and no limits.
And that Love is for you and for me.

One day, as I was picking up trash in the backyard of our newly acquired inner city building, Samuel, an elderly gentleman came out of his house and sat down on his porch. I greeted him and he invited me to join him. After introducing myself, he offered me a seat on an upside-down plastic bucket, which I eagerly excepted.

As we talked, he asked what we planned to use the building for. I shared our vision to reach the children in this neighborhood with the message of the gospel.

The creaking of his rocking chair stopped, he leaned toward me and said, *"I knew it! I've told my son many times that building has a high purpose. Why, that old building has such a history. It's seen many hard times. I was born right here in this old house back in 1910. That building was there before I came into this world. I've watched many businesses move in, stay awhile, then move on to greener pastures. That building's been through fire and flood waters. But look at it, it's still standing and will probably still be standing when we're both dead and gone."*

I looked at the old, red brick building with its boarded-up windows. I saw the blackened bricks on the second floor where years before a homemade gas bomb was thrown in the window in an effort to burn the place down. Yes, I had to agree that this old place had many stories to tell, if only walls could talk.

Samuel took up his conversation again. *"There are two rival gangs in this neighborhood. The street your building faces is the dividing line between the two gangs. One is called, the 'Bloods' and the other is the 'Crypts'. The Bloods control the territory on the opposite side of the street facing your building and the Crypts control the territory on this side of the street and behind us. These two gangs have been fighting for territorial rights over your building and the corner it sits on for over a year now. It was the strangest thing to me that neither gang ever got control of it. Finally, after fighting for so long and neither side winning, the two rival gang leaders came together just a few months ago and decided to declare your building and the corner it sits on as 'neutral territory'. The night my son came home and told me that, I told him right then and there that God must have big plans for that place. I ain't never heard of the Bloods and Crypts agreeing on anything much less giving up an opportunity to have a good fight and gain new territory. But now that I hear what you plan to use it for, well, I reckon I was right. God done looked down the road and saw you comin', so He prepared this place for you just like the good book says. The way I see it, God done took care of what would've been a big problem for you. So, you just go on and do what the good Lord's put in your heart to do and teach these kids. And God bless you as you do."*

* * * * * * *

The full impact of what I'd learned that day didn't really dawn on me until several months later.   I watched children from the Bloods' side of the street cross over to the Crypts' side of the street eager to learn about this man Jesus. I went inside the building and sitting on the front pew was the four-year-old brother of a Blood gang member with his arm around the five-year-old brother of a Crypt gang member. There was no gang-turf here, only 'God-turf' as the children call it. There's no fear in this place. And in this place, the siblings of rival gangs and sometimes gang members themselves sit together, praying, singing, learning and laughing together—just like family.

Coop and the author.

CHAPTER TWENTY-THREE

Coop

Little children,
Let us not love with word or with tongue,
But in deed and truth.
I John 3:18

We cannot place a value on what we do for another,
Only the one receiving our gift can know its true worth.
Often, it's the simple things that make the greatest impact

𝕵ust down the street from our inner city ministry building, lives an elderly lady. Her name is Mrs. Cooper, or 'Coop,' as she's called by everyone who knows her. When I asked her how old she was, she replied, *"Why, child, don't you know you don't ask a lady a question like that?"*

With a wink, she smiled and added, *"So, just how old do you think I am?"*

"I'd guess around sixty-five?"

She laughed and her deep, chocolate eyes danced with delight. She replied, *"Well, cause you're so gracious, I'll forgive you for asking."* She leaned close and whispered, *"Don't tell anybody, but I'm eighty-something. I won't tell you what the something is, though."*

I would've never thought she was in her eighties because of her endless energy and amazing spunk.

I asked Coop if she had any children, she hesitated a moment then answered, *"No, my husband and I never did. He was diagnosed with a terminal illness right after we were married. He was bedridden for many years. I did all I could to ease his suffering. When friends suggested I divorce him and remarry so I could have a family, I told them to take a hike. When I said my vows promising to love him in sickness and in health until death do us part, I meant it! And that's just what I did right up to his passing. After that, I never remarried cause I never loved anyone like I loved my husband."*

After her husband died, Coop chose to stay in their home. She worked as a school librarian and loved being with the children so much that she worked there until her sixty-seventh birthday. After she retired, she was offered a job to be a nanny for a doctor and his wife who had two young children. She jumped at the opportunity and for the next ten years she loved and cared for those children. On her mantle are numerous photos of these two children, who Coop claims as her own.

Coop also spent her life pouring love into the neighborhood children. *"After all,"* she says, *"that's the way it was in my day. Everyone watched out for everybody else. If a child was getting into trouble in front of your house, why, you just went out there and straightened him out. When you were done with him, then you went down and told his mother and she'd thank you and make sure he got the message. That's just the way it was. Neighbors took care of neighbors. We really cared about each other and about our neighborhood. Now a days, it's not like that and I believe that's what's wrong with this neighborhood. Folks just don't care about each other. They come home and go straight into their house and their kids just run around all day with nobody to watch after them. It ain't right, I tell you, it just ain't right. Children need to be loved and taught what's right and wrong. It just ain't right the way things are now a days."*

To fully appreciate Coop's strength and personality, I must tell you about my first encounter with her. It was nearly five years ago and quite a rare experience for me, but then Coop is quite unique.

It all began one Saturday as I was sweeping glass off the sidewalk in front of our newly donated ministry building. We had plans to start a children's outreach called, 'Kid's Explosion' in this neighborhood and I was very nervous about how we'd be received by the community. After all, we were outsiders and most of our volunteers were white, coming into a predominately Afro-American community. The more I swept, the more I thought, and the more nervous I was getting. What did I think I was doing?

I leaned against the building. The bricks were warm against my back. The sun was shining with all its strength; however, the air was quite cool. I thought of going inside, but instead I shut my eyes and allowed the warmth of the sun and bricks to warm me. The hectic traffic noises, dogs barking and the various sounds of busy day-to-day life grew distant and dim. My thoughts carried me back to a day in March; the year was 1964.

My family had just moved from town into the country. I had to leave behind my very kind second grade teacher, Mrs. Royal. This was very traumatic for me. If that wasn't bad enough, I had to ride a school bus for the first time and go to a new school. My only comfort was that my older brother and sister were with me.

We arrived at the school and I was left alone to locate my classroom. This school wasn't anything like my old school; this school was huge. I stood frozen in the hallway with children laughing and talking all around me. No one spoke or even seemed to notice me.

I had no idea which way to go. The school bell rang causing my anxiety level to go from about six to a definite ten. I wondered what teachers in this school did to children who were late for class. My eyes filled with huge, alligator tears. I wanted to run away, but didn't know where to go.

I looked up, just in the nick of time and caught a glimpse of my brother at the far end of the hall. With everything that was in me, I ran to him. I never once thought about the fact that this was the same brother who was a 'meany' nor did I think about the fact that he was the one I picked on and teased incessantly. Nevertheless, at that moment in time, he was real close to looking like an angel!

I stopped just short of knocking him over. He took one look at my tear-drenched face, immediately took my hand and without saying one word helped me find my classroom. That was a day I never forgot.

The sun and bricks had warmed me, but not as much as the memory of my brother's kindness. He'd made all the difference in the world to that frightened, little girl. My brother saw me through a very traumatic event. Even though it happened thirty-five years ago, I still remember as if it was yesterday. That's the power of kindness.

With renewed faith, I opened my eyes and once again, surveyed my present surroundings. Nothing had changed. I was still a stranger here, an outsider. I still felt vulnerable. And yet, I had renewed hope. I prayed and asked the Lord to send someone to take me by the hand, just like my brother had and lead me through the initial getting acquainted process.

A few minutes later, I saw an elderly lady walking towards me. I decided it would probably look better if I was busy, so I quickly picked up my broom and resumed sweeping. A few minutes later, this lady walked directly up to me, got right in my face and asked, *"What're you people doin' here?"*

Without waiting for my response, she continued, *"I don't allow no riffraff in my neighborhood. Just what're your plans for this building? Are you opening a bar here? Are you going to be serving liquor here? Just who are you folks, anyway?"*

This wasn't exactly what I had in mind when I asked for someone like my brother to help me. I leaned back against the wall for support, took a deep breath and gave it my best shot, *"My name's Rhonda and my husband's a pastor. We're going to use this building to hold bible clubs for the children in this neighborhood."*

Instantly, her stern expression changed and a big smile covered her face. Grabbing my hand and shaking it quite energetically, she replied, *"You're Christians! Well, child, why, didn't you say so? That changes everything! You see, it's like this, my name's Coop and I watch out for this neighborhood. Nothing goes on around here without old Coop knowing about it. I always have my say about it, too. This has been my home for over fifty years. I make sure nobody comes in here and brings trouble. We don't allow no riffraff in our neighborhood. That's why I came down here to see what you're all about. But since you're Christians— well, welcome to the neighborhood!"*

I laughed out-loud from sheer relief. As if we were old friends, she took my hand in hers and we walked around the neighborhood while she told me about my new neighbors. Once more, God had come to my aid.

The following week we were cleaning out the basement when Coop came in; her eyes were dancing. I greeted her with a hug and she excitedly said, *"I just came from our monthly neighborhood meeting. I told them all about you folks. I told them who you are and why you're here. I also told them that you're good folk and they should welcome you. They listen to old Coop, so you shouldn't have any problems here."*

Coop opened her arms wide and embraced us, leading the way for others to do the same. But that wasn't the end of Coop's contribution to us. When we began Kid's Explosion, she informed us she'd be at all of our meetings. She said, *"I know these kids. They need a firm hand as well as lots of love. So, I'll be here every week to help you."*

She kept her word. Every Saturday morning, Coop showed up wearing a great big smile and a baseball cap embroidered with the phrase, 'Christmas in October.' I asked about her hat. She said, *"Why, I believe a person should celebrate Jesus' birth everyday of the year—and I figure October's just as good as December."*

Coop often talked about how things were 'in her day'; how families and schools have disintegrated. She spoke of how much her neighborhood has changed in just a few years. It distresses her to witness most people living for themselves and not caring about others. But mostly, she grieves over the way so many parents allow their children to wander the streets. She fears where America is headed because so many have laid aside their Christian values for self-values. She really worries about the children—and she's not alone.

* * * * * * * *

This past year, Coop has had to slow down due to her failing health. However, she's still a fireball and continues to love the children who knock on her door.

CHAPTER TWENTY-FOUR

Dynamite Comes in Small Packages

Owe nothing to anyone except to love one another;
For he who loves his neighbor has fulfilled the law.
Romans 13:8

It isn't an address that makes someone
your neighbor—it's a caring heart.

𝕮oop and I quickly became good friends. I looked forward to seeing her each week. Recently, she and I were standing in front of the ministry building talking and enjoying the beautiful sunshine, when a car stopped rather abruptly in front of us. An elderly gentleman leaned across his seat and rolled down the passenger window. In a very stern voice, he asked, *"Are you the person who's responsible for this building?"*

"Yes, sir," I replied.

With harshness, that caused me to brace myself, he said, *"I've got a complaint against you."*

Instantly, before I could respond, Coop stepped in front of me like a lioness protecting her cub. She put her hands on her hips and asked, *"Don't I know you?"*

Stepping off the curb and leaning her head into his car, she said, *"Yeah, I know who you are. You live on the street behind my house. But that don't make no difference. You can't come over*

*here with that kind of attitude. I know these folks and they're good
people. Did you know they drive all the way down here several
times each week to teach the bible to **our** children? They teach
them about God. They hug them and hold them in their laps and
love them. They wipe their runny noses and wash their dirty faces.
They listen to them and correct them when they need it. They bring
them clothes and food. They even take some of them home with
them on the weekends and treat them like part of their family. So,
don't you come driving up here and complaining one little bit about
these folks. If you want to complain, why you just go find some
place else to do it cuz old Coop just ain't gonna stand for it!"*

The gentleman held up his hands in defense and in a much
nicer tone said, *"Whoa! I guess I was a bit harsh. I just wanted to
tell these folks that the bushes on the back fence block my vision
when I pull out of the alley. I just want them to cut those bushes
down. And as far as what they're doing for the children, well,
that's great, but they still need to take care of any potential hazards
for other people."*

I assured him we'd clear the fence right away. He thanked me
and quickly drove off.

Coop put her arm through mine and as we strolled toward her
house, she said, *"I guess he got quite an ear full of old Coop. I
wasn't about to stand there and let him give you a good thrashing.
People need to look for the good in folks and not be so quick to
complain about 'stuff.' Stuff just ain't as important as folks make it
out to be. This world would certainly be a much better place and a
lot more peaceful if folks would set their minds on things that really matter, the things that really count. And I ain't talking about
some bushes growing on a fence."*

I had to laugh at this little woman standing beside me. She
definitely fit the saying, "Dynamite comes in small packages."

That day, I felt that I *really* belonged here, like I was part of the
neighborhood. As I walked Coop home, I thanked her for standing
up for us. After all, I was the new kid on the block. I was the
outsider, but then again, maybe not.

* * * * * * * * * *

Needless to say, Danny cleared the back fence that same day.

Part VI

SUFFER THE LITTLE CHILDREN

Jesus said, "Let the children alone,
And don't hinder them
from coming to Me,
For the kingdom of heaven
belongs to such as these."
Matthew 19:14

THE LITTLE ONES

There are little hearts
That are broken.
There are little bodies
That are battered.

There are little minds
That are confused.
There are little tummies
That are hungry.

And, there are little souls
Waiting to hear
That there is a Savior
Who loves them.

How can they come, if they aren't invited?
How will they be invited, if we don't seek them out?
How can they be sought out,
if we don't go where they live?
How will we go where they live,
if we don't love them the way Jesus did?

Jesus said, *"...don't hinder them from coming."*
— Rhonda

CHAPTER TWENTY-FIVE

The Day Heaven Kissed the Children

And everyone kept feeling a sense of awe...
Acts 2:43

Who can comprehend the ways of God?

Kid's Explosion is a bible-based, fun-filled, discipleship program for children. Volunteers pass out flyers in the neighborhood, inviting the children to come have fun while learning about Jesus. Our purpose is to build Godly character, love unconditionally and teach bible truth.

Our song leader was teaching the children a new song this particular Saturday morning. We were all concentrating intensely as he taught the hand motions. I suddenly noticed that seven-year-old Victoria had gotten out of her seat and was sitting on the floor across the room. I knelt beside her and saw that she was crying. I asked what was wrong. She was sobbing so hard that she couldn't answer. I asked if she was sick or if someone had done something to hurt her. She shook her head no. I held her in my arms and waited until finally, between sobs, she blurted out, *"I'm crying because people are dying and going to hell!"*

That wasn't the answer I expected. I asked Victoria what she thought she should do. She said she wanted to ask everybody to pray for these people to believe in Jesus. That sounded like a good idea to me. We waited for the song to end, then I took Victoria's hand to help her up, but her legs were shaking so much that she could barely stand.

As I practically carried her to the front, the whole room became completely silent as the tangible presence of God filled the room. There were more than forty young children in the room and not one of them moved. At that moment, I was trying to decide whether I should try to speak or just fall on my face.

Victoria continued to weep. I decided to explain why Victoria was crying. As I did, children all over the room began to cry. Victoria fell into a heap at my feet, weeping harder than ever. There was such a strong sense of God's presence in the room that my knees buckled and I landed beside her. I was afraid to look up. It was as if the Lord Himself had walked into the room. At that moment, I was keenly aware of my many imperfections in the presence of such an awesome God.

All over the room, we prayed with our tears. Every child in the room sat with their eyes closed, nearly every one of them had tears pouring down their face.

I watched as three-year-old Dee-Dee scooted off the front pew and knelt down on the floor. As I write this, I struggle to find words to describe the beauty and purity of Dee-Dee's worship. There she was a tiny three-year-old, who'd never been to a 'church' service in her life, bowing before God with her hands clasped together in prayer-like fashion under her chin. Tears of love ran down her cheeks. (To this day, this touches me deeply.)

It was as if an unseen Hand moved about the room leading the children to follow Dee-Dee's example. Quietly, the children knelt anywhere they could. All that could be heard was the sound of crying. It was intense, yet sweet. The weeping ebbed and flowed like the ocean waves, with a rhythm all its own. It became a song from the hearts of these children to the heart of their Father—a song for the lost.

In the middle of all of this, an older gentleman walked in and sat down beside Coop. That's when I noticed the two back pews were filled with men and women. I'd never seen them before and they weren't there when we started. For a brief moment, I was concerned about what they'd think. After all, it's not everyday one sees this many children bowing, kneeling or lying face down sobbing, for no obvious reason. I thought about going to them and trying to explain what was going on, not that I fully understood myself, but quickly dismissed the thought. I didn't want to miss out on what God was doing in our midst. Besides, even if I wanted to go to them it would've been very difficult to make it across the room through the sea of bodies.

Children from the ages of three to thirteen were experiencing a touch from God in a tangible way, totally unaided by man. The conductor of this orchestra was God. After some time, some of the Kid's Explosion workers began moving among the children, asking how they could pray for them. Several said they needed Jesus, but many asked for prayer for an unsaved relative or friend. There wasn't one child or adult in the room that was unaffected by the sweet presence of the Lord.

Sitting on the floor near me was an eleven-year-old boy. His eyes were fixed on a distant point and his face looked pained. I asked what was going on and he answered, *"I was just thinking that I should do better in school. No, that's not true. I was thinking that I should be nicer at school. No, that's not true, either. I was really thinking that I should stop being so mean to my sisters."*

His eyes filled with tears and he quickly covered his face. Other children began confessing their sins. And through it all, little Victoria continued to bow before her God.

For just over three hours, no one left, no one went to the bathroom and no one asked for food or drink. Normally, our program is approximately ninety minutes long; then we pass out candy and prizes to the children, ending with lunch. On this day, their hearts were so gripped by God that they thought of nothing except God and the lost.

Then, just as suddenly as it began, it ended. It was as if someone snapped his fingers and the crying stopped. Some of the children remained on the floor, praying for a little while longer. The others quietly tiptoed outside and waited on the sidewalk.

When the last child got up from the floor, I went outside. There were several children leaning against the wall and some others were sitting on the sidewalk. I wondered what they had to say about what had happened. I saw eleven-year-old Derek, so I asked him what he thought.

Derek answered, *"It was the best."*

I asked him why and he replied, *"Because Jesus was here."*

"How do you know Jesus was here?"

He looked at me as if I had just landed here from Mars and replied, *"Because I saw Him. He was standing in front of me and walked right up to me and put His hand on my shoulder."*

I asked if Jesus said anything and he said, *"Nope, He didn't have to, it was enough that He touched me."*

What an incredibly, interesting answer.

Just then, I remembered the men and women who were sitting on the two back rows. I went looking for them. They were no where to be found and no one had noticed when they left. I asked Coop if she knew who they were. She said she'd never seen them before today. We talked about how odd it was that they just walked in off the street. How'd they know to come inside and why today? I had so many questions and no answers.

One of the unique things about this 'event' is that these children weren't raised in church. However, on that day, it mattered not how much they knew or didn't know about God. It only mattered that they were there.

And we all experienced God in a very real and tangible way.

* * * * * * * * * *

The children talk about that day often; they refer to it as 'the day heaven kissed us'!

The little worshiper, Dee-Dee sitting with the author.

CHAPTER TWENTY-SIX

Is This My Church?

On this rock I will build My church;
And the gates of Hades shall not overpower it.
Matthew 16:18

A CHILD'S CRY

To belong, to be a part of a family that loves me,
To be part of something that's good and right.
Is it within my reach? Is it even possible?
Or am I just reaching for the wind,
Or grasping for an elusive butterfly that quickly flies away?

𝕵ust a few months after we began the children's outreach in the inner city, Danny and I arrived early to prepare for a party we were having for the children that day.

Six-year-old Shalonda was the first to see our van. She was busy playing in her front yard, but she quickly dashed across the street. Running into my open arms, she gave me a big hug. Her face glowed despite the dirt smudges on her cheeks.

Within minutes, several other children appeared from various places in the neighborhood. Numerous little arms reached out to give and receive hugs. Shalonda, being somewhat timid had retreated from the crowd. After everyone was hugged and the children scattered, I looked around for Shalonda.

She was leaning against the wall of our ministry building watching me. She looked so fragile and needy, another victim of the poverty that's rampant in this inner city neighborhood. My heart ached for her. I knelt down beside her. Putting my arm around her skinny little waist I whispered, *"I love you."*

That was all she needed. Her arms flew around my neck and she squeezed me so tightly and energetically that I lost my balance. She maintained her iron grip and we both toppled over laughing as we landed on the sidewalk. I took advantage of the situation and tickled her; she exploded into squeals of laughter. I stopped to allow her to catch her breath; I looked into her beautiful chocolate-brown eyes. She's so sweet and so innocent, I thought. How will she ever make it in this crime filled neighborhood?

We helped each other up and then Shalonda walked over to the brick wall and patted it asking, *"Is this my church?"*

Taking her thin hand in mine, I answered, *"No, sweetie, this isn't a church. This is where we have Kid's Explosion."*

She patted the wall again and with more intensity asked, *"But, is this my church?"*

Once again, I responded, *"Sweetie, no, this is where we have Kid's Explosion."*

This time she slapped the wall and with great intensity asked, *"I know that! But is this **my** church?"*

I asked myself why this was so important to her. This little girl standing before me, in all practicality, didn't have a thing to call her own. She had no idea who her father is or where he is. Her mother disappeared when she was just a tiny baby. She was left with her grandmother, who was already raising several other grandchildren. Her grandmother couldn't imagine how she'd ever take care of another, but took her anyway. Shalonda's living conditions are very poor, having no bedroom to call her own. She and her four cousins share the same room and they take turns sleeping on the one and only cot in the room. Her clothing is handed down from her older cousins. But, in spite of it all, she's still so tender and sweet.

As I looked into her pleading eyes, I understood that Shalonda was crying out to know she belonged. This building represented love and acceptance. In this building, Shalonda had met someone who loved her just like she was and His name was Jesus. I asked myself what was a church anyway? It certainly wasn't a building. A church is nothing more than a group of believers who gather to worship God and love each other. This seven-year-old somehow understood this truth and wanted to know if she was part of it or not. She'd found a place where she was loved by God and by people. She'd found a church and this building represented that to her. Cupping her chin in my hand, I patted the wall and said, *"Yes, Shalonda, this is your church."*

Her face lit up like a Christmas tree. She threw both arms around my neck and said, *"I'm so-o-o glad!"*

She planted a big kiss on my cheek, and then just as quickly as she came she left, a content little girl.

* * * * * * * * * *

As for me, I left that day, with a deeper understanding of church.

An apprehensive Derek goes for his first horseback ride.

CHAPTER TWENTY-SEVEN

Will Anyone Help Me?

A father of the fatherless
And a judge for the widows,
Is God in His holy habitation.
Psalm 68:5

There's a silent cry that's much louder than words.
Can you hear it?

Meet Derek. He's eleven-years-old. If he's lucky, Derek sees his father once a year. His thirty-one-year-old mother uses drugs and alcohol regularly. Three of her thirteen children are already in prison. Derek is the main caregiver for his seven younger brothers and sisters. Everything about life is hard for this little guy.

We first met Derek at Kid's Explosion. He walked to the ministry building with his brothers and sisters following closely behind him like little ducklings. He marched them right in and sat them on the front row. Derek planted himself in the middle to make sure they behaved.

One Saturday, we invited all the children to come back the next day to join us for a special church service and to stay for lunch. Sunday morning turned out to be a bright, sunny day. I could hear the birds through my open bedroom window singing their clear, sweet songs in anticipation of a great day. I was eager to get downtown.

As we drove, I asked the Lord to remind the children about the service. We turned the corner and there was Derek leaning against the building with his hands stuffed in his pockets. His not-so-white shirt was buttoned all the way up to his chin and was haphazardly tucked into his much too small jeans. One of his worn-out tennis shoes was missing its lace. However, his face was glowing and his little family stood behind him eagerly waiting for the adventure that lay before them. After all, it wasn't everyday they get to dress up in their Sunday best and go to church.

I was so thrilled to see them and told them so. Derek excitedly said, *"I got up extra early this morning cause it takes a lot of time to get these guys ready. I gave them a bath and got them dressed cause I didn't want to be late—we even got here before you. We're goin' to have lunch like you said, right? We don't have nothin' to eat at home."*

I assured him there'd be more food than they could possibly eat.

During the service, Derek tried his best to keep the little ones quiet. Believe me, it was quite a task, so several adults gladly helped by holding the younger ones. Derek was quite the little man through it all.

Lunch was served and Derek filled a plate for each of his brothers and sisters. I offered to help, but he said he could do it. He brought each of them a drink and cautioned them not to spill. He made sure they were settled before he went back for his lunch. This little guy knew what he was doing and I was quite impressed.

Derek quickly became one of my favorites. He was always eager to help and really enjoyed the bible stories. Derek could barely read. He made sure we repeated the memory verse several times, so he'd be able to recite it the following week. Over the next six months, Derek began to smile and we even had him laughing out loud a few times. He even went from being emotionally frozen to becoming one of our best huggers.

Then, about a year into our relationship, something happened. From one week to the next Derek went from being happy and loving to being withdrawn and unresponsive. Several Kid's Explosion workers tried to find out what was going on, but Derek wouldn't say a word to anyone. Anxious to find out what was happening, I walked him home and talked with his mother. She said, *"He pulled a knife on a kid at the bus stop. So, he can't ride the bus anymore and I can't take him to school. He's going to spend the rest of the year right here helping me. I just don't know what to do with that boy."*

Two weeks later, a terrified Derek watched as his mother was brutally beaten by her boyfriend. This had happened before. But, this time, Derek and his thirteen-year-old brother Tyrone couldn't restrain themselves. Tyrone was the first to speak up, and Derek joined him. The boyfriend stopped his assault just long enough to let them know if they didn't shut their mouths, they'd be next. He then walked over to the television, picked it up and threw it on the floor, busting it at their feet.

Derek was helpless to stop the insanity happening in front of him. The rage consuming him threatened to explode from his little body. Afraid, he withdrew to the far corner of the room and planned what he'd do to this man when he was big enough. Tyrone fled from the house. A couple hours later, Tyrone ran into our ministry building. It was Friday night and the youth group was in the middle of their meeting. It was obvious Tyrone was extremely upset. Tracy, the leader, asked what was wrong. He told them what had happened and that he was going to get a gun and kill the guy. Two of the other leaders went to check on Tyrone's mother. Without being asked, the teens quickly gathered around Tyrone. His friends and peers talked about what he should do. They encouraged him to forgive the guy, even though he didn't deserve it. Then, they prayed for him and his family. That night, what had been a disjointed group of inner city teens, who occasionally had fights of their own and normally repaid violence with violence, became a loving, caring, sympathetic group. They cried, hugged, and earnestly prayed together on behalf of a hurting, distraught teenager who had no other place to go. They didn't stop until Tyrone prayed and asked God to forgive his mother's boyfriend. Many tears fell that night.

(Tyrone went home with one of the leaders and ended up living with them for the rest of the summer.)

The next day, I visited Derek who was still extremely angry. He said, *"Do you know what it's like to watch your mom get the crud beat out of her and you can't do nuthin' about it? Well, I do and I'm gonna get that guy when he ain't lookin'. He won't ever hurt my mom again."*

"Derek, I know you're really hurting right now. But, believe me, hurting him will only hurt you. There's a better way."

"The only better way would be if I was outta' here. I gotta' get outta' this place," Derek said.

"Derek, why'd you pull that knife on that kid at the bus stop?"

He answered, *"I'll tell you why. I want somebody to notice how bad it is for me. I can't stand it here anymore. And I'll tell you something else, I'm gonna' keep getting into trouble until somebody gets me outta' here."*

I had nothing to say. After a few minutes, he looked me right in the eye and asked, *"Do you know anybody who'll help me?"*

Who would be willing to take a severely troubled eleven-year-old? I had no idea. We already had one inner city teenager living with us. I had no clue who to ask. It's difficult to find people willing to open their homes to these troubled children. Yet, I couldn't ignore his desperate cry for help. As soon as I arrived home, I called our intercessors and asked for their prayers.

The following morning, when I woke up, I immediately thought of our friends, Bob and Mary. Maybe, just maybe, they'd be able to take him; they're wonderful, loving Christians who are faithful to do what God asks. I called and shared Derek's situation with them and asked if they'd prayerfully consider giving him a home at least for the summer. They agreed to pray. The next day, Bob and Mary called with the good news; they'd take him!

The next hurdle was Derek's mother; we needed her permission. We told her about Bob and Mary and their offer for Derek to spend the summer on their farm. Without asking one question, she quickly and eagerly consented. The last hurdle was Derek. Was he serious about getting out? Would he be willing to leave the city and go so far away? I found Derek and told him about Bob and

Mary. I described the farm to him and some of the fun things he'd get to do like fishing, bike riding, horseback riding, and summer camp.

His only question was *"When do I leave?"*

We arranged to pick him up on Monday morning. I wondered how he'd adjust to such a drastic change. After all, he'd never been away from home or even outside the city. He was accustomed to taking care of his many brothers and sisters. Would he miss them too much? He'd be going from an extremely noisy, hectic, chaotic, violent life with no boundaries to a farm with no neighbors, no traffic, no yelling, no fighting, and no children to take care of. For the first time in his life, he'd have rules and boundaries. This was definitely going to be a drastic change.

The next day, Derek ran up to me with his hands behind his back. He had quite a mischievous, little grin on his face as he said, *"I have a surprise for my new family."*

From behind his back he brought out a birdhouse and said, *"I found it in a trash can. I know it's not the best in the world, but do you think they'd like it?"*

I held it in my hands and examined it. The bottom was missing, the perch was broken, the hanger was rusty and bent, and the blue paint, what was left of it, was old and very faded.

I looked back at Derek's beaming face and said, *"This is the neatest birdhouse I've ever seen. I'm certain that Bob and Mary will absolutely love it."*

With much enthusiasm, he exclaimed, *"YES!"* then asked, *"Will you keep it in your van? I just know it'll get stolen if I keep it here."*

I was honored to be the keeper of the birdhouse.

Monday morning came and we arrived at his house at 9:15 to find him sitting on the top steps alone. Tucked under his arm, there was a paper bag packed with a pair of shorts, one shirt, a pair of swimming trunks, a toothbrush and a blanket. Cradled under his other arm was a bag with several plastic worms he'd bought for twenty-five cents at a yard sale.

Running to our van, he said, *"I thought you weren't coming."*

He threw his stuff in the back seat and climbed inside. I asked where his mom was. He said, *"She's still in bed. I told her I was leavin' and she mumbled something. I'm ready, let's go."*

We drove off. He never looked back.

We had a four hour drive ahead of us. The first two hours, Derek talked non-stop. He said, *"I got up at 3:00 a.m., dressed, brushed my teeth and put my bag on the porch. I was afraid I'd miss you guys. I sure didn't want that to happen."*

He talked about everything he saw along the roadside. He was very curious and asked many questions about cows, horses, silos, fishing ponds, corn, bales of hay, etc. Finally, for the first time in two hours, there was complete silence. I turned around. Derek was stretched out on the seat, sound asleep. We stopped for lunch and I tried waking him, but he didn't move. I decided anyone who could sleep that deeply must need the sleep more than the food so I left him alone. We bought him lunch, thinking he'd wake soon. Not quite an hour later, he woke with a start, *"Are we there, yet?"* He asked.

Danny and I laughed, asking him if he was hungry. Within minutes he devoured his cold lunch. Just as he finished, we arrived at the farm. The first thing in sight was a large barn, complete with cows. Not too far from the barn stood a rather large shed with steps leading up to a door. Derek pointed to the shed and asked if that was his new home.

"No, Derek, that's the shed. Look over there across the yard. That's your new house."

His eyes grew large. The white farmhouse was beautiful with its wrap-around porch, swing and dozens of rose bushes in full bloom. Behind the house were numerous bales of hay sitting lazily in the field. On the far side of the house was a vegetable garden, surrounded by a white picket fence. And in the distance, on all sides, the farmhouse was surrounded by God's beautiful handiwork—rolling hills and lush valleys.

Derek's eyes were huge and his grin was even bigger as Danny parked the car. Derek quickly grabbed his bag, jumped out and ran to the front door. Catching up with him, I rang the doorbell. As the door opened, Derek quickly ducked behind me, suddenly timid. I put my arm around him and introduced him to Mary. She lovingly embraced him, then asked if he'd like to see his new home. I'm not sure whose smile was the biggest, Mary's or Derek's.

From his excitement, you would've thought he was in Disney World. Mary saved his bedroom for last, knowing he'd never had a bedroom of his own. He ran in and sat on the edge of the bed to check out the springs, just like they do on television. We all laughed.

We left Derek in his room and went downstairs. He followed shortly thereafter with birdhouse in hand. Somewhat timidly, he handed Mary his priceless gift saying, *"I got this for you."*

Mary excitedly thanked Derek for his gift. Derek then said, *"I know it's not great, but maybe we could paint it or something."*

Mary then told Derek she had a surprise for him and led him to the dining room where numerous gifts were waiting. Mary had wrapped his gifts in plain white paper and had placed 'Jesus loves you' stickers all over them. I thought his little face was going to break from grinning so much. Item by item, he opened his gifts, then very carefully put them back in the boxes. He thanked her, then asked if he could put the wrapping paper on the bulletin board in his room. When she said he could, he jumped up and said, *"I'm not ever leaving here."*

Having completely explored the inside of the house, Derek wanted to see the outside. The rest of the day was spent exploring the farm. We explored every inch of the barn, found treasures in the shed, identified wild animal tracks around the pond, climbed the hay bales, fed the cows, checked out the tractor, explored the woods and all it contained. We rode the bicycle, tasted the deer's salt block (and discovered it was awful), chased a hawk circling overhead, closely inspected the insides of a crushed turtle, tasted honeysuckle, and climbed up in the hayloft (again). We joined him for his first family meal, had a nerf war with Bob, made up songs on the guitar, and swung on the porch swing while thousands of locusts serenaded us.

Bedtime came and Derek suddenly told us about an abusive situation he'd suffered at the hands of his mother's boyfriend. Bob and Mary assured him he was safe with them. We barely had the covers tucked around him before he fell asleep.

Danny and I spent the night. Derek's room was across the hall from ours. I tossed and turned unable to stop thinking about the day. I prayed for a while, then got up. Tip-toeing across the hall, I stood in his doorway. The moonlight spilled in through the window softly shining on Derek's sweet little face. He was lying on his side, with his hands tucked in prayer-like fashion under his cheek. He slept peacefully.

I looked around his room. On the desk were the presents Bob and Mary had given him, each one perfectly displayed. He'd covered his bulletin board with the 'Jesus loves you' wrapping paper. His basketball peeked out from under his bed. His football bedspread was tucked under his arm. This was a typical boy's room, although, Derek wasn't your typical boy. He had many deep wounds and some serious problems to overcome. It would take much patience and great love to see him healed. I was grateful that Jesus had more than enough of everything this little guy needed.

I thought back to the day at Kid's Explosion when Derek saw Jesus walk up and lay His hand on his shoulder, the shoulder of a fatherless boy. And now, so many months later, here he was sleeping in a home filled with unconditional love and kindness.

Derek was safe in this place and safe in His Father's arms.

* * * * * * * *

Derek lived with Bob and Mary throughout that summer. Much love was poured into him and he thrived. But sadly, he was unable to stay and had to return home.

CHAPTER TWENTY-EIGHT

Because You're Cryin'

Rejoice with those who rejoice
And weep with those who weep.
Romans 12:15

Beautiful faces, loving hearts-
innocent children surrounded by evil.
Children abused and neglected by the world we live in.
How do we sleep at night?

$\mathfrak{I}$t was the 4th of July and we were having our annual community barbecue in the inner city. I made my rounds in the neighborhood, collecting the children. I felt like the Pied Piper as I skipped down the sidewalk, a group of children skipping around and behind me. It was an absolutely beautiful day; the sun was shining and the birds were singing. Turning to the children I said, *"Let's sing our memory verse!"*

With quite a diversity of musical ability, we sang loud and clear as we skipped along. I had a feeling this was going to be a great day! We crossed the street behind our ministry building and immediately came to an abrupt stop. Lying beside a tree was a large bouquet of red roses. They were dry and shriveled. I stared in silence. The children were silent as well.

After a few moments, eight-year-old Keith said, *"Them roses are there cuz a man died here 'bout two weeks ago."*

I knelt down and touched the brown, crisp petals. *"How did he die?"*

With no emotion, as if he were giving a book report, Keith answered, *"I saw the whole thing. It was Thursday and I was playing in my yard when this guy came walking down the street. I don't know who he was cuz I ain't ever seen him before. Anyway, this guy said something to the two dudes who live over there."* He pointed to the house across the street. *"I couldn't hear what he said but whatever it was, they didn't like it. In a flash, they jumped over their fence and ran after him. They tackled him and threw him on the ground. Then they beat him. One of the dudes busted a whiskey bottle in his face. He fell on the ground and they just kept beatin' him until he quit movin.'"*

At this point, I began to cry. I cried because of the senseless loss of a life and for these innocent children who were subjected to things most of us only see on television or read about in the newspaper. I cried for Keith, an eight year-old who witnessed such a violent act and talked about it with no emotion whatsoever. Children should never be subjected to this type of thing.

The children had knelt down around me and I looked at their beautiful faces. None of them seemed to be fazed by this. How would they ever survive all the violence that surrounds them? And what other horrors would they witness and, even worse, what horrors would they personally experience in the years ahead?

Interrupting my thoughts, nine-year-old Sue pushed her way through the children, then knelt beside me. She asked, *"Rhonda, why are you crying?"*

I took her sweet, little face in my hands and answered, *"Susie, I'm crying because someone died and he was killed right here in your front yard. And I'm crying for you. I'm sad you live in a place where this kind of evil happens and I'm sad that your neighborhood isn't a very safe place for you."*

I kissed her forehead, then whispered a prayer for these sweet children.

Having said amen, our ever so practical Keith responded with, *"I'm really hungry. Can we go eat now?"*

Mustering up a smile, I nodded and we resumed our walk. But, as hard as I tried, I found it impossible to stop crying. Sue took my hand in hers. Our joyful walk had turned into more of a funeral procession. No one was singing and no one was laughing. We continued in silence. We hadn't gone far when I realized Sue had tightened her grip on my hand to the point that it was hurting. I looked at her and saw tears streaming down her face. Stopping, I knelt down in front of her and looked into her deep brown eyes, *"Why are you crying, sweetie?"*

She took my tear-drenched face in her little hands and simply replied, *"Because you are."*

Her words hit me like ice water on a steamy day. This little girl still loved; she still felt. Oh, how beautiful she was! Beautiful, not just because of her physical features, but beautiful because of her heart. My grieving heart exploded with love, joy and peace! I scooped her off the ground and swung her around. I began to laugh. Not at her, but I laughed in the face of an enemy who thought he was more powerful than love. I laughed at an enemy who thought he could destroy children by filling their world with violence, destruction and hatred. I laughed because this incredible little girl had risen above it all. Despite her environment, she still loved and she still cared. I laughed because of hope. Hope for Sue and hope for the many other children in this neighborhood and the thousands of other neighborhoods just like this one. This precious little girl, full of wonderful love and simple goodness, was an example of the incredible power of love.

Still laughing, I put Sue down and wiped the tears from her face. She then wiped the tears from my face. She took my hand in hers as we continued on our journey.

* * * * * *

For weeks after, we filled the neighborhood with our song of hope: *"Seek first the kingdom of heaven and all shall be added. They say we need money and power. They say there's no God up above. Don't they know our God in high places? **Nothing can be stronger than love.**"* That song has become a favorite of ours.

Sue poses with Day-z the Clown, who is the author's daughter, Dana.

CHAPTER TWENTY-NINE

Mercy Triumphed

Blessed are the merciful, for they shall receive mercy.
Matthew 5:7

Jesus said that whatever measure you use to judge another
That same measurement will be used to measure you.
Sobering thought, don't you think?

On a snowy January day, David, one of the teenage leaders of a gang called The Blood's walked his little brother to Kid's Explosion just as he'd done for the past six months. As usual, David stood guard outside the door waiting to walk his little brother home. We invited him to wait inside where it was warm. But, as was his custom, he politely refused.

"If you change your mind just open the door and come on in," I said.

I shut the door and asked God to drive him inside by sending more snow. About twenty minutes later, the door opened and in walked a very cold, snow-covered teenager. He sat on the back row. Taking advantage of the situation, I changed what I'd planned to teach, thinking this may be his only chance to hear the gospel.

We talked a lot about how Jesus is merciful and how, in His great compassion, He set us free from our sins. We talked about the cross, heaven and hell and unconditional love. David appeared to be listening, he hardly moved. At the end, I asked if anyone wanted to accept Jesus as his or her Savior. He shifted in his seat and leaned forward as several children raised their hands. As I led the children in a prayer of salvation, David bowed his head—his lips moved! Afterwards, I said, *"David, I'm so glad you came inside. I must confess that I prayed God would cause it to snow harder, so you'd come inside."*

"Why would you do that?" he asked.

"Because I care about you. I wanted you to hear that Jesus loves you and to have an opportunity to give your life to Him."

He didn't respond. I said, *"You know, this is the most important decision you'll ever make in your whole life. Don't wait until it's too late. Do you understand?"*

He nodded, then said he had to go.

The following week his little brother came to Kid's Explosion alone. I asked where David was. He answered, *"He told me I could come by myself now cause he said angels were with me and they'd protect me."*

From then on, his little brother came alone.

Six months or so passed. Jerod, one of the teens from our Friday night Youth Explosion, came home with us for the weekend. As we ate chili-cheese fries, (Jerod's favorite food) he began to talk about his life.

He said, *"After I gave my life to Jesus I couldn't go back to my old ways. So, I had no choice but to tell my gang brothers I wanted out. The problem is nobody gets out of a gang without paying the price. I knew it was the right thing to do, so I went into that meeting with my knees knocking and told them I wanted out. They asked me why I was being so stupid. Well, the next thing I know, I'm telling them all about Youth Explosion and my decision to follow Jesus. Man, I was so scared my voice was cracking and my whole body was shaking. Every chance I got I was begging God to help me. You could've knocked me over with a feather when they said I was free to go."*

"Jerod, why'd they do that?" I asked.

He answered, *"Because of one of the leaders. I don't know*

him very well, but he stood up for me. After I was done telling them about how Jesus changed my life, this dude named David stood up and said, 'I think we should show him mercy. I know it's not the way we do things around here, but maybe we should give him a break. You never know, maybe if we take it easy on him, someday somebody might take it easy on us. How many of you have enough bad stuff going down in your life that you'd love somebody to show some mercy to you? Yeah, that's what I thought. Well, Jerod needs some mercy real bad right now. He's up against the wall for something he believes in and I think we should show the dude we got a heart.'"

Jerod continued, *"I couldn't believe it! After that you could've heard a pin drop in that place. And man was I sweatin' while they took the vote. Everybody voted to let me go free. Man, was I glad. Believe me, I thanked Jesus all the way home and for a long time after that."*

* * * * * * * * * *

I laid in bed that night wondering if David, the leader that spoke out in defense of Jerod was the same David who came inside on that snowy January day and heard the story of a Savior who died to set him free. Somehow, in God's wonderful economy, I suspect that's exactly what happened.

CHAPTER THIRTY

The Love of a Child

At that time the disciples came to Jesus, saying,
"Who then is greatest in the kingdom of heaven?"
And He called a child to Himself and
set him before them, and said,
"Truly I say to you, unless you are
converted and become like children,
you shall not enter the kingdom of heaven."
Matthew 18:1-3

Jesus loves the little children, all the children of the world.
Red, yellow, black and white, they are precious in His sight.

Danny and I were busy cleaning the ministry building downtown. Danny was picking up trash in the back lot when seven-year-old Tina ran across the street. In her cheerful way, she skipped right up, threw her arms around his neck and squeezed him tightly. He hugged her back.

She said, *"I've got a surprise for you."*

She pulled out a piece of candy and a sticker from her pocket. She took his great big hand in her little one and pressed an orange piece of candy in it. She then proceeded to peel the backing from the sticker and pressed the sticker on his shirt pocket.

Danny gave her another hug, thanking her. He asked where she got such a wonderful piece of candy and such a cool sticker.

She answered, *"My teacher gave me four pieces of candy and four stickers cause I was good this week. I ate one piece and put one sticker on my notebook. I saved the rest to give to the three people I love."*

In her hand there were the two remaining pieces of candy. Danny's eyes filled with tears. He was overwhelmed with a myriad of emotions as he thought about what she'd said. Tina asked, *"Where's Rhonda?"*

Regaining his composure he answered, *"She's in the Kid's Explosion room."*

As she turned to head my way, Danny grabbed her hand and said, *"Tina, thanks so much for sharing your goodies with me. That was very special. I want you to know that I love you, too."*

She smiled. Her two front teeth were missing, which only made her more adorable. She squeezed his hand then ran off to search for me.

The door opened and I looked up to see the cutest little girl running towards me. Her face was alive and her eyes sparkled. She had a multitude of tiny braids in her hair with various colored barrettes strategically placed all over her head. She was wearing jean shorts, a purple T-shirt and no shoes. Her clothes and face were quite dirty, but who cared? I got down on my knees and wrapped my loving arms around her tiny frame. What a great feeling! After a few moments, Tina pulled back and said, *"I got somethin' for you. Somethin' very special just cause I love you."*

She pulled out of her pocket two pieces of candy and two stickers. She gave me a red jawbreaker and stuck the sticker on my shirt. Thanking her, I put the candy in my mouth and asked if she was going to eat the last piece.

Quite alarmed, she answered, *"Oh, no, I'm not gonna' eat it! My teacher said I was so good this week that I could have four pieces of candy and four stickers. Well, I done ate my piece of candy at school. I had three pieces left so I decided to give them to the three people I love. I gave Danny one and I just gave you one. And, this piece, I'm saving for Jesus just as soon as I see Him."*

What love! What faith! I was speechless and tears filled my eyes. *"Don't you like your candy?"* she asked.

"Oh, yes, sweetie. It's the best candy I've ever had."

"Why are you crying then?"

"Because you're so beautiful, that's why. These are happy tears, not sad ones. I think it's so wonderful that you love Jesus and I so much that you'd share your candy and stickers with us. Thank you, sweetie."

There was no doubt in her mind, that Jesus was just as real as Danny and I. She knew she'd see Him one day and when she did she had something to give Him.

* * * * * * * * * *

I left that day so much richer because of a sticker on my shirt and a piece of candy in my stomach. My faith was challenged because of a precious little girl who loves Jesus, Danny, and me.

CHAPTER THIRTY-ONE

Stop, Look and Listen

And so, as those who have been chosen of God, holy and beloved,
Put on a heart of compassion, kindness,
humility, gentleness and patience.
Colossians 3:12

It takes time to notice pain.
It takes time to see and hear their cries.

𝕴t was the summer of 1996 and we were starting a Kid's Explosion in another low-income apartment complex in the suburbs. It was our first meeting and approximately thirty children sat on the blue tarps, as the Kid's Explosion team diligently worked to reach their hearts and minds. The children sat without moving. Their faces were expressionless. They seldom laughed or smiled. Nothing we did excited them—not the clowns, the music, nor the games. Not even the prizes. We'd never seen such emotional emptiness in a group of children before. Our team left that day committed to lovingly break through the walls of indifference and hopelessness that held them prisoners.

Over the next several weeks, our team poured love into these children. We talked and asked questions about anything and everything, trying to win their trust and affection. Slowly, signs of life began to show on their little faces. Over the next several months,

most of them became loving, excited children who, when they saw
our team drive up, would eagerly run to greet us with hugs and
laughter. It was very exciting to see these caterpillars turn into
beautiful butterflies right before our eyes.

But sadly, during the course of the year, I became so busy with
the business of running a ministry that I forgot to look into the
children's eyes. I forgot to listen. We had won their trust and
affection, so I had relaxed. I find that it's easy for me to lose ground
when I get comfortable because my senses get dull and I begin to
function on autopilot. Thankfully, a little girl named Christy awakened me from my complacency.

That Saturday, we'd given each child a candy bar, a pack of
gum and a small box of cereal. Most of the children had gone
home and we were busy packing our supplies. I was in a hurry
because I had an appointment in less than an hour. In my rush, I
only half-noticed Christy sitting on the curb all alone. The fact she
was still there and that she was alone should've set off my warning
bell. But in my haste, I missed the signals and kept going full-
steam ahead.

A little later, as Danny and I were folding the tarps, I noticed
Christy still sitting in the same place—still alone. My second
chance, but I shrugged it aside.

I was boxing up the leftover cereal when suddenly two dirty,
little bare feet appeared beside my box. I quickly glanced up at
Christy and smiled. The box of cereal we'd given her was tucked
securely under her arm and the candy bar was held tightly in her
hand. I was surprised she hadn't eaten them. Very quietly she
asked, *"Could I have another box of cereal, please?"*

I continued packing the cereal and replied with my standard
answer, *"I'm sorry, but we only have one for each child and if I
give you two boxes then all of the other children will want another
one."*

I looked up. Her big, blue eyes filled with tears and her chin
was quivering. Her nose was sprinkled with tiny freckles, the evidence of being kissed by the sun. Dirt smudges covered one cheek.
She wore a winter sweater that was much too small for her (it was

summertime). Her bright, blue shorts were very old and tattered. She slowly turned and walked away. Why was she crying? Immediately, it occurred to me **what** she'd asked for. We'd given out candy bars and cereal, but she hadn't asked for candy. I ran after her. I took her hand in mine and asked, *"Are you hungry, sweetie?"*

She answered, *"Just a little, but I've got five brothers and sisters who're more hungry than me."*

Oh, how beautiful she was and how wretched I was! I put my arms around her and said, *"Everything's going to be all right. I'm really sorry for telling you no about the cereal. I was just too busy and I wasn't thinking with my heart. But, let's fix that. I was wondering if you could help me out? You see I have this big box full of cereal and I don't have the time to take it home. So, I was wondering if you'd help me out by taking it home with you? Do you think you could carry a box this big?"*

Her whole face instantly lit up as she answered, *"I'm sure I can carry it! I know I look small, but I'm really very strong."*

"You sure are—in more ways than one, sweetie," I replied.

That week, I did some investigating and learned that Christy and her five brothers and sisters lived in a two-bedroom apartment. Their mother used drugs and a steady stream of boyfriends come and go at all hours of the night. All of the children had different fathers, none of which claimed them. The children slept on the floor in one bedroom.

Having learned this, we took food and clothing to this family. Their mother let us in then went back to bed. Her children jumped up and down, squealing with excitement as we put the food and clothing away. Before leaving, we cooked a meal for them, making sure they were full.

The next week, I looked with open eyes at the other children in this complex. Many of them wore clothes that were out of season and in very poor condition. We decided to begin a monthly clothing give away. We decided to make it a celebration and gave away hot dogs, chips, cookies and soft drinks to any and everyone. It became quite an event as many of the children's parents came and we were able to get to know them. Several adults gave their lives to Christ and several prodigals came home through this outreach. It was all because of a little girl, who taught me to stop, look and listen.

* * * * * * * *

Soon after this, Christy and her siblings were placed in foster care.

Part VII

CHRISTMAS MEMORIES

THE PERFECT GIFT

Long before I was born
You were laid in a manger.
And, even then, You knew me
And loved me with all Your heart.

A baby lying in a crude wooden box
Sleeping between two sheep,
Became my Savior hanging on a wooden cross,
Dying between two thieves.

First a stable—then a tomb.
Both times His mother looked on
And wondered, "How can this be?"
His virgin birth—now His unbelievable death.

In the cold, dark tomb lay the Perfect Gift
Sent to a most imperfect world.
God's beloved Son, the Lamb of God
Despised—rejected—now dead!

Why? How? For what purpose?

Your answer came swift and clear
On that resurrection morning,
"I died that you might live,
For Love pays the price."
— Rhonda

CHAPTER THIRTY-TWO

My Most Memorable Christmas

Mercy triumphs over judgment.
James 2:13

Thankfully, we have a heavenly Father
who is merciful and kind.

𝕴n December 1970, I was thirteen-years-old. I laid on my bed looking out the window at the crisp, night sky. The moon shone in its fullness and a multitude of brilliant stars decorated the endless sky. I desperately tried to block out the conversation going on just outside my door. Yet, as hard as I tried, the words blasted me like a bitter, icy wind. My mother was telling my older brother and sister, *"There'll be no Christmas again this year. Your father drank up all the money. There's nothing I can do...."*

I pulled my pillow tightly over my head, trying desperately to block out any further news. It seemed unfair we should suffer so much. Our lives had been a series of one painful event after another. *"Somehow,"* I told myself, *"this Christmas won't be like all the others."*

I didn't know what I was going to do, but I was going to do something.

The weeks passed and the Friday before Christmas, my mother and I drove into town to pick up my sixteen-year-old sister from

205

work. My mother sat in the car while I went window-shopping. As I looked at all the wonderful gifts, I thought about my family and Christmas morning. There'd be no tree to decorate, no gifts to open, and no Christmas dinner. I looked around at all the people rushing from store to store; their arms were filled with beautifully wrapped gifts and their laughter filled the air. My grief grew to an unbearable proportion. I must do something! So, with tears streaming down my face, I walked into a store and discreetly picked up a paper bag. Carefully selecting just the right gifts, I slipped them into my bag. Then, I walked out. The store manger was waiting for me. She was very angry as she grabbed me by my long hair and dragged me into a back room to wait for the police. To my horror, my mother was summoned and shortly thereafter the police officer arrived. He asked a lot of questions, then took the manager aside and asked her not to press charges. But, she was adamant I pay for my crime.

I made the traumatic trip to the police station, where I was again questioned. I was told I'd have to appear before the juvenile judge and he'd decide what would be done with me. I had no idea what that meant, which created even more terror for me.

On the drive home, my mother pointed out the error of my ways and made sure I understood the magnitude of what I'd done. I was thoroughly embarrassed, ashamed and devastated; my conscience was speaking loud and clear. I was keenly aware I'd displeased my heavenly Father and the weight of my sin pressed down and threatened to crush my very tender heart.

The church I'd grown up in taught that publicly committed sins must be confessed publicly. Because I wanted to do what was right, on Sunday, I walked down the church aisle (it had to be at least five miles long) to confess my sin. With each step, I grew more ashamed and my sobbing filled the place. After what seemed like forever, I made it to the front and quickly sat down. The preacher knelt in front of me. Without daring to lift my head, a torrent of words poured out of my mouth and a river of tears ran down my face. He listened, then stood and announced to the church my confession.

That was supposed to be the end of it, or so I thought. I was supposed to walk out of there forgiven and restored. It didn't happen that way for me. The congregation was dismissed. No one approached me. No one reached out to me. No one spoke to me, and no one gave me the hug I so desperately needed. The pain in my heart intensified, as I felt further isolated. I ran from the church and felt the brand of thief seared onto my heart forever. Shame filled every part of me. I waited in the car for my family and our long drive home was spent in silence. As soon as the car stopped in front of our house, I ran straight for the field. Throwing myself into the knee-high grass, I sobbed and sobbed.

I was alone. Well, not really. My heavenly Father who loved and accepted this weak and sinful, but eager-to-please, little girl met me there. I poured out my grief to Him and His peace filled me. He assured me that I was forgiven and not only forgiven, but loved.

The weeks passed slowly, finally it was time for my court appearance. My mother asked our preacher to go with us. We were escorted into the judge's lavish chambers. The judge dressed in the finest clothes I'd ever seen sat behind a huge, highly polished, mahogany desk. We sat in silence as he read the police report. Removing his glasses, he asked my mother, *"So, what kind of student is she?"*

"She's a good student, she makes straight A's."

"Does she give you trouble at home? What about school?"

"Until this incident, she hasn't been in any trouble at all. She's always been an obedient child."

"Are you her father?" He asked pointing to our preacher.

"No, sir, I'm their preacher."

"What kind of girl have you found her to be?" He asked.

"She's always been a quiet, well-behaved girl."

The judge sat back in his magnificent chair, one hand rubbed his chin and the other drummed on his desk. After a few minutes, he said, *"I don't quite understand. I don't believe I've ever had a child in my court that did something like this without having previous warning signs either at home or at school. And, yet, from what you're telling me it sounds as if she's been in no other trouble be-*

fore this shoplifting incident. Is this true?"

"Yes, sir, that's exactly right," my mother replied.

The moment I was dreading happened; he turned his attention to me. Instantly, tears filled my eyes. Leaning forward, he asked, *"So, Rhonda, why did you steal these things?"*

Without thinking, a flood of words poured out, *"My father's an alcoholic. He drank up all the money, which meant we wouldn't have Christmas. So, I stoled those presents for my family. I know it's wrong."*

His eyes were fixed on me for much too long. Finally, without saying a word, he shuffled through the stack of papers in front of him and read out-loud the list of items I'd stolen. Looking at me over his glasses, he asked, *"So, what items on this list did you steal for yourself young lady?"*

I was shocked by his question! Not for a moment had I considered taking anything for myself. I replied, *"Nothing!—I didn't steal anything for me!"*

That's when the raging river broke through the dam and I sobbed as the pain and shame of the past weeks poured out.

The judge now leaned forward, extended a box of tissues to me and smiled for the first time. Once I calmed down, he turned to my mother and in a very firm voice said, *"Don't you punish this child!"*

He then turned to me and said, *"Not guilty! I find you not guilty. You're free to go—and remember, don't ever steal again— no matter what."*

I couldn't believe it! I'd never experienced forgiveness like that! The judge extended mercy to me, when I deserved punishment. He'd seen my sin, but didn't camp out there. Instead, he looked beyond my actions to the unseen motives of my heart. Upon seeing the whole picture and being a compassionate judge, he chose to extend forgiveness. Just like my Judge and Father in heaven.

* * * * * * * * * *

That Christmas, I received a gift I will never forget, a gift I will never outgrow. The precious gift of forgiveness, forgiveness from man and from God.

I rejoice knowing there will be another day, when I'll stand before a Judge again. But, it will be the great judgment seat of God. On that day, I'll take no confidence in anything I've done or haven't done. My only assurance will be in the blood of Jesus that washed away my sins and brought me into His family. And based on that truth, I'll hear the Judge of all judges say, *"Not guilty! I find you not guilty. This child isn't to be punished for anything she's done or hasn't done."*

Not because of me, but because of His great mercy.

James on his last birthday.

CHAPTER THIRTY-THREE

I'll Do Anything

In everything, I showed you that by working hard in this
manner you must help the weak and remember the
words of the Lord Jesus, That He Himself said,
"It is more blessed to give than to receive."
Acts 20:35

Christmas means loving and giving.

One of the hardest stories for me to write was, without a doubt, the preceding chapter, 'My Most Memorable Christmas.' In writing it, the deep shame of that dreadful event overwhelmed me. But, for God's glory, I want to share how God used that story to heal and set me free from the shame that I've carried for nearly thirty years.

When I began to write the Christmas section of this book, I found myself thinking back to that painful Christmas. I felt a familiar nudge that I was to write about it. However, I'd put a lot of time and energy into forgetting what I had done and had absolutely no plans of sharing it with anyone. My shame was still too great. Yet, no matter how hard I tried, I couldn't quit thinking about it. Frustrated, I turned my computer off.

For several days, I wouldn't go near my computer. Then, my husband reminded me I needed to write our monthly ministry newsletter. Not wanting to face the pain that was lying just under the surface, I answered him quite sharply. Later that afternoon, I realized I was going to have to deal with this hurt and shame once and for all. It was time. Staring at my blank computer screen I prayed, *"Help me, Lord. I want to be brave, but I'm not. Actually, I'm very scared to tell this story."*

Reminding myself of Psalm 56:11, *"Lord, in You, I put my trust, I shall not be afraid. What can man do to me?"* I started writing. In no time at all, the story was written. I printed a copy for Danny to read and afterward he said, *"Let's use this as our newsletter this month. After all, it's a Christmas story."*

With great anxiety, I agreed to do so. I can't describe the terror I felt when over 400 newsletters telling my horrible story were sent out to friends and family.

I thought I'd get up in the morning and feel better, but I didn't. Three days later, while shopping, I saw one of the pastors from our church. Not realizing my shame and discomfort and thinking he was encouraging me, he talked in much detail about the newsletter. I could barely look at him and couldn't wait to get away. I left the store absolutely convinced I'd just made the biggest mistake of my life in sending out that newsletter. I couldn't change the fact that I'd mailed it out, but I could certainly remove it from this book, which I planned to do.

Desperate, I prayed, *"Lord, I feel awful. I'm so ashamed. I need Your help."*

His answer came quickly and in a way I never expected. The very next day, a week before Christmas, James, a twelve-year-old from our inner city Youth Explosion came up to me during the break at church. One look at his face and I knew something was very wrong.

I asked, *"Are things bad at home, again?"*

He nodded yes.

"You want to talk?"

Again, he nodded. We went outside and sat on the church steps.

"Okay, buddy, what's going on?" I asked.

With head down, he answered, *"We don't have any food at our house. It's not so bad during the week 'cause we have free lunch at school. But, my brother and me haven't eaten since Friday. Last week, our stove and refrigerator was repossessed 'cause my mom couldn't keep up the payments. She found a used refrigerator yesterday, but it took her whole paycheck to buy it. Now she doesn't have any money to buy food to put in it."*

Putting my arm around him, I said, *"James, don't you worry one more minute; Danny and I will see that your refrigerator is filled this afternoon. How does that sound?"*

"That's really great, but..." he stopped in mid-sentence.

"Go ahead, James. Is there anything else?"

"Well, my mom told me and my brother she won't be able to buy us anything for Christmas cause she doesn't have any money. Well, that doesn't matter so much to me, but it sure matters to my little brother. I was wondering if you had some jobs I could do so I can buy my brother and mom a Christmas present? I'll do anything."

His words, *"I'll do anything,"* cut through me like a knife. I understood the desperation he felt all too well. It felt like I stepped back in history. *"This time,"* I said to myself, *"there will be a different ending."*

Putting my arm around him, I answered, *"James, I'm so glad to know that you're available to work. I just happened to have several jobs that desperately need to be done. Let's go ask your mom if you can come home with us after church and you can get started right away."*

He quickly went inside. I turned my eyes to heaven. *"Thank You, Lord for allowing me the awesome privilege of doing for this family what I so wish could've been done for me so many years ago. Oh, how I love You for it!"*

In that moment, sitting on those cold church steps, it no longer mattered to me if 400 or 400,000 people knew what I'd done so many years ago.

James first job was to put together about thirty bags of groceries from our food pantry and help us deliver them to his mother. Then, he was given several other jobs to do. Every chore was done with excellence. We then left for the store. He agonized over each gift, making certain it was just right. After finding several for his mom and brother, he then asked Danny and I to leave so he could buy us something. (He chose a screwdriver set for Danny and a musical manger scene for me.) We watched him walk out of the store with a big grin on his face and a bounce in his step.

After he was settled in the back seat with his packages all around him, I asked, *"James, I was just wondering—did you buy anything for yourself?"*

"No way, this isn't about me!" he replied.

"Somehow, I thought you'd say that."

Then, I told him my Christmas story and in the telling, my shame and guilt completely melted away.

The next day, I called some friends and told them about James and his family. They happily agreed to 'adopt' them for Christmas. They bought Christmas presents and provided them with food for a tremendous Christmas feast.

On Christmas morning, James walked to a pay phone and called me. He gave me a detailed description of all the wonderful Christmas presents he, his brother and mother received. Then he said, *"I loved everything I got. But, watching my mom and brother open the presents I bought for them—that was the best part. Thanks for the best Christmas I've ever had. I'll never forget it."*

Neither will I. And this time it ended just right.

* * * * * * * *

The story doesn't end here. This past Christmas, James' mother received a bonus at work, which she used to help a family who was in need just like she'd been. The love goes on. . . .

CHAPTER THIRTY-FOUR

Cuz He Loves Me

Thou hast given him his heart's desire,
And Thou hast not withheld the request of his lips.
Psalm 21:2

Because He cares
Absolutely nothing, absolutely no one can escape
God's listening ear, His watchful eye, His gentle hand,
His loving heart, or His wonderful ways.

𝕋eron sat cross-legged in the corner of the room among a group of about seventy children. At the other end of the room was a mountain of beautifully wrapped Christmas gifts, each with the name of a child taped to it. Even though the room was packed with so many very excited children, there was no way I could miss seeing this little guy. He sat on the floor rocking and repeating something over and over. I carefully made my way through the mass of children and sat down beside him. I leaned close and heard him say, ever so quietly, yet most intensely, *"Oh, I hope I get a car and I hope it's a fast car!"*

My husband began passing out the gifts and Teron folded his little hands under his chin in prayer-like fashion and continued his pleading. His heart was crying out with such passion, that I knew this would be one of those Christmas memories that would either be a major disappointment or a major delight.

My daughter and I had wrapped most of the presents and I had no idea which gift had been wrapped for this little guy. It was too late to do anything, except pray. I joined Teron in asking God for a miracle.

Finally, Teron's name was called and he ran to receive his gift. He returned holding a brightly wrapped box close to his little body. Our eyes met and we both smiled. His eyes danced with a mixture of anticipation and uncertainty as he sat down beside me. He closed his eyes tightly and whispered for one last time, *"Oh, **please**, let it be a fast car."*

With that last plea, shreds of paper flew everywhere as he excitedly tore into his gift. Teron shot straight up, as he exclaimed, *"Look! I got a car and it's a fast car!"*

He was holding a very fast-looking police car. Teron had received his miracle. With a big sigh, I whispered, *"Oh, thank You, Lord."*

Teron handed me the box and said, *"Will you tell me about it?"*

I asked, *"Do you want me to open it?"*

"Oh no," he answered, *"I just want to look at it. Just read it to me."*

Teron climbed into my lap and I read every word printed on the box. I pointed out the working headlights, the siren, the flashing red and blue lights, and the doors that really opened. He ran his hand slowly over the wrapper as if it was a priceless treasure, then whispered, *"Now, will you open it for me?"*

"Most certainly, my friend."

I lifted the police car out of its box and laid it in his waiting hands. He stood up and held it out for me to admire. Never, in all of history, has a police car ever been treated with such tender, loving care. He displayed it from every possible angle and pointed out every feature to me, then said, *"I prayed for a fast car and God gave me the best!"*

"You're right, Teron, God gave you the best! Do you know why He did that?"

He answered, *"Yep, I sure do. He gave me the best cuz He loves me."*

* * * * * * * * * *

Teron was exactly right and God gave us His best 2,000 years ago because He loves us so very much.

A happy Teron.

CHAPTER THIRTY-FIVE

The Perfect Gift

Every good thing bestowed and every perfect gift is from above,
Coming down from the Father of lights,
With whom there is no variation, or shifting shadow.
James 1:17

A perfect gift should never be rejected.

We'd just finished serving Christmas dinner to about eighty inner city children, most of them were regular attendees of Kid's Explosion. The level of anticipation in the room increased noticeably as we announced it was time to hand out the presents. Every eye focused on the mountain of colorfully wrapped gifts that were waiting to be put into the arms of a child. I looked around the room at all the precious little faces eagerly listening for their names to be called. So many children with so many hopes! I was completely enthralled with the drama unfolding before me.

Across from me, four-year-old Shaneqa sat Indian-style on the floor at her mother's feet. She wiggled with hopeful anticipation, waiting for her special moment. Even though it was a very cold December night, she was wearing a faded, sleeveless dress. Around her chubby little neck hung a piece of yarn with a single yellow bead. On her feet was a pair of old terry-cloth slippers that were more than ready for a plot in the shoe cemetery. Her hair was an intricate design of many braids held fast by quite an assortment of brightly colored rubber bands. Her bright eyes and beautiful smile were as lovely as a daisy to me.

Shaneqa patiently watched as the children around her opened their presents. With the unwrapping of each gift, her eyes grew bigger and she'd inch just a little closer. She was definitely growing more anxious as the mountain of gifts shrunk. Then, with only a handful of gifts remaining, her name was finally called, but surprisingly she didn't move. Instead, she looked at her mother and waited for permission. The nod came and away she ran with arms extended to embrace her gift.

She returned with a box that was wrapped in white Christmas paper and had a very large, red bow at its heart. She sat at her mother's feet and looked up, waiting for the nod that would give her permission to discover what great thing was hidden in the box. The nod came, bringing a smile to her face. She very carefully removed the paper revealing a plain, white shoebox. She lifted the lid; inside was a pair of very fuzzy, pink slippers. Lifting the shoes out, she flung the box aside. Sadness swept over me. Thinking there had to be a toy inside that box, I walked over and looked. The box was empty.

I couldn't bear to look at Shaneqa, so I looked around the room instead. All of the other children were playing with their toys, so many toys and so many happy faces. I couldn't believe it. Who would give a four-year-old a pair of slippers? Little girls love things like baby dolls, teddy bears, books, and tea sets-not slippers.

When I dared look back her way, I couldn't believe my eyes. She was grinning from ear to ear. I watched as she rubbed the slippers against her cheek, giggling because the fuzz tickled her nose. She lifted them eye level and watched with fascination as the fuzz swayed in response to her every breath. Then, she put them on her hands, pretending they were puppets and had them twirl and dance all over her knees.

After Mr. and Mrs. Puppet finished their show, she hurriedly stepped out of her old slippers, replacing them with her new ones. Then, she danced. Like a miniature ballerina, she danced. She became her own music. Precariously, she stood on her tiptoes and reached for the sky. A sweet smile appeared on her little face. She twirled and twirled some more. For the grand finale, she crossed her ankles and curtsied. I could almost hear her imaginary audience explode with applause.

What a performance! How beautiful, how graceful! Not once did Shaneqa ever look around to see what the other children had or what they were doing. She was content with what she was given. She loved her gift and that made it perfect.

That was good enough for me. I learned something that day.

As the months went by, Shaneqa continued to enjoy her gift. She wore those slippers inside and outside. She wore them in the snow and in the rain. She wore them even after her big toe pushed its way through the end. I don't think there's ever been a Christmas gift loved more than those slippers. But, the day finally came when she had to part with them. She laid them in my lap and asked, *"Can you fix them?"*

I took them in my hands and said, *"I don't think so sweetie. I think it's time for a new pair."*

She said, *"But, they were my Christmas present."*

What could I say? I tried explaining, but I wasn't very successful. When it was time for her to go home, I filled her pocket with candy then walked with her. Just as we arrived at her porch, she turned and said, *"Do you think I'll get another pair at our next Christmas party?"*

"Shaneqa, it wouldn't surprise me at all if you did."

The next day, I bought her a pair of pink, fuzzy slippers just like her old ones. I could hardly wait for Saturday's Kid's Explosion. When she unwrapped her present and saw the shoes, she asked, *"Is it Christmas?"*

Laughing, I answered, *"No, sweetie, it's not Christmas. I just wanted to give you these shoes because you are such a special little girl, who I love so much. And, besides, everyday is Christmas with Jesus, Shaneqa."*

* * * * * * * *

In writing Shaneqa's story, I couldn't help but think about how Jesus is our Perfect Gift. He was presented to mankind inside the walls of a stable and was tucked away in a crude, little feeding box, (similar to a plain shoebox, if you will). He didn't choose to be born in a mansion, even though He was royalty. Instead, this King was content to live as a common man. He was content with simple things and simple ways.

But, the people of that day weren't content. They were looking for a bright, shiny Messiah, not a common carpenter. They looked in the box and demanded a toy. They wanted more. But, there were some who embraced Him as the gift that He was. They found eternal life. They found God.

Today you can still receive and embrace this Gift sent from heaven. There's no need to look around and see what everybody else has. There's no need to look for something better because He's the only perfect gift there is or ever will be. He's all you need.

Jesus chose to live a simple life. He was content to live as a homeless man, a commoner. Imagine that, the Son of God choosing to live as a common man when He could've lived in extravagant wealth and power. Instead, He became less that we might be more. He died that we might live. No one forced Him. No one talked Him into it. He wanted to die. His love is greater than we know. He couldn't stand the thoughts of spending eternity without *you*—that's why He died.

"Truly I say to you, whoever doesn't receive the kingdom of God like a child shall not enter it at all." Mark 10:15. I read this passage and think of Shaneqa and the child-like way she accepted her gift. You can do that, too. Jesus can be like those brand new slippers. You can throw away your old shoes, your old way of life and step into a new way of life with Him. This Gift never grows old and never wears out.

Jesus is alive and He loves you deeply. Accept Him today as the Son of God. Give him your life, both your past, your present, and your future. He'll wash away your sins and give you eternal life. He'll see you through the hard times and He'll rejoice with you through the good times.

Your decision today determines your destination tomorrow.

CHAPTER THIRTY-SIX

Do You Love Me?

Therefore be imitators of God, as beloved children;
And walk in love, just as Christ also loved you,
and gave Himself up for us,
An offering and a sacrifice to God as a fragrant aroma.
Ephesians 5:1-2

It's so much easier to love a child than it is to heal an adult.

𝕴t was early Christmas morning, Danny and I were awakened by the sound of excited voices filling our basement apartment. I could hear eleven-year-old Molly and ten-year-old Kaitlin giggling. The two sisters had moved in with us four months earlier. Shortly after, Dewayne, a nine-year-old boy in crisis joined our family.

We hurriedly dressed. Our 'little family' went upstairs to celebrate Christmas with Fred and Barb, the couple who so graciously share their home with us. Everything was decorated so beautifully. The Yuletide log burned, carols filled the air, and beautifully wrapped presents waited under the Christmas tree.

My heart overflowed as the gifts were passed out and the children began opening their gifts. In the midst of all the excitement, Kaitlin unwrapped a doll. Ignoring her other unopened gifts, she cradled this new doll in the crook of her arm. Something about the adoring look on her face made me think of another young girl who

223

lived approximately 2,000 years ago. I wondered what Mary felt as she held her first-born. What thoughts filled her mind as she looked into His eternal eyes? Mary knew He wasn't an ordinary baby; she knew His conception was miraculous. Did she trace the outline of his tiny face with her fingers and think about the day when her life was forever changed—the day an angel appeared announcing that she'd give birth to God's only Son?

"Your name is Jesus," she whispered with great reverence. Smoothing the dark hair that covered His head, she continued, *"The angel told me you'd be a king and would sit on David's throne and that your kingdom would never end. I wonder how you will ever go from sleeping in a manger to ruling on a throne?"*

Mary tenderly watched over the Creator and Savior of the world as He slept on a bed of hay. For the next thirty-three years, she pondered the words spoken by the angel. On the day He died, still wondering about those words, she stood at the foot of His cross gazing at His battered body. Tenderly, Jesus looked down at his mother. Love and compassion filled His being. Turning His pain-filled eyes to John, He said, *"John, my dear friend, take good care of my mother."*

He gasped for breath as He turned His thorn-pierced head toward His mother, *"Mother, John will care for you as a son."*

Sobbing, Mary collapsed at the foot of His cross. She looked for the last time into the eyes of her son. Her heart cried out for understanding. How could this be happening? The angel said He'd be a King and His kingdom would never end. So, why, how could this be possible?

Closing her eyes, she fell against John as he held her close. This mother, who heard the Son of God's first cry, now heard His last. *"It is finished!"* he cried.

Mary looked into John's eyes. Somehow, some way, Jesus will become King and He will reign forever. I'm sure of it, she thought.

The ground began to shake and weary Mary clung to John. The soldier in charge of the execution fell to his knees and cried out, *"Surely, this was the Son of God!"*

Just then, Dana laid her hand on my shoulder and said, *"Mom, something's wrong with Dewayne."* I looked around. Kaitlin had resumed her gift opening. Molly was ripping open a large box. Dewayne was no longer opening his presents, but sat quietly on the couch.

He was handed a gift, which he slowly opened, then quickly laid aside. Something was definitely wrong. Another present was given to him, yet he barely responded. Danny and I compared notes as to what could be wrong.

Just two weeks before, he'd told us the only thing he really wanted for Christmas was a scooter. But, he was quick to say they cost too much. Later that night, Danny and I discussed his desire for a scooter. We felt strongly that we should buy him one, even though we'd already bought him several gifts. We asked the Lord to provide the money. Just two days later, we were given a check for more than enough to buy the scooter. Danny bought one in Dewayne's favorite color and hid it in the garage.

Our plan was to give it to him last, but it seemed Dewayne was so disappointed about not getting a scooter that he was unable to enjoy his other gifts. Danny suggested we go ahead and give it to him.

I sat beside him and handed him a small, square box that he slowly opened. I whispered, *"Dewayne, what's inside this box is meant to show you just how much we love you. We want you to know that you're very important to us. Every time you see this gift, remember we love you very much."*

He lifted the lid to discover a note inside that read, "Your scooter is in the garage." He looked at the paper, placed it back in the box, then laid it aside. I was shocked! Maybe his distress had nothing to do with the scooter after all. Then, I remembered his poor reading skills. Picking up the paper, I whispered, *"The note says that your scooter is in the garage."*

It took a moment for the words to sink in. Then, he asked, *"What'd you say?"*

I repeated the words. Instantly, he jumped up and literally fell into me, hugging me more tightly than I ever thought possible. His body began to shake as he sobbed in my arms. His whole body became limp as disappointment fled from his heart. His tears quickly soaked my shirt. Oh, how he clung to me! I could feel him accepting my love. This was the first *real* hug he'd ever given me and probably the first one he'd ever given anyone. I whispered repeatedly how much we loved him. After quite some time, he left to hug Danny, then Dana, crying all the while. Then, he returned to me once more, still crying, and held me as if he'd never let me go.

It was as if he'd forgotten all about the scooter. I asked if he'd like to see his new scooter. He grinned and answered, *"Sure."*

Danny brought the scooter in and Dewayne wiped the tears from his face and neck. *"I just can't believe it! You really bought it! I never thought anybody'd ever do anything like this for me!"*

Later he said, *"I told myself I'd know if you loved me if I got a scooter for Christmas."* Tears filled his eyes as he continued, *"When I looked at the presents and there wasn't one big enough to be a scooter, I was so sad cause I thought you didn't love me."*

Dewayne and I talked quite awhile. It was good. We ended with talking about how Jesus paid the ultimate price (much more than the price of a scooter) to show us how much He loved us. And what does He ask in exchange? All He asks is that we love Him and love others. Such a simple requirement-especially considering the cost!

* * * * * * * *

I've thought quite a lot about Dewayne and his desperation to know he was loved. As anxious as he was to be loved, he found it impossible to believe it could be true. We'd done everything we knew to do, but couldn't break through. Our love had to be proven— in this case, something as simple as a scooter did it. We're not much different from Dewayne; we long to know God loves us. Without this assurance, we constantly try to fill the emptiness in our hearts. Oh, how very important it is for those of us who know and have experienced the tremendous love of our Father to be diligent in demonstrating His Love to others. How do we do that? By following Jesus' example—we lay down our lives.

After all, isn't that the true message of Christmas? Isn't that what the birth of our Savior was really about? He was born so He could die and in doing so, He paid the price and proved His love for us. His life was a message that's still heard today: *"I came because I love you. No one forced me to leave the splendor of heaven, no one talked Me into it and no one paid Me. I came because I wanted to. I came not only to tell you of My love, but also to show you. In doing so, I paid the ultimate price. And I died not only for My friends, but also for My enemies. Dear ones, you're worth the price I paid. You're worth it all. And I love you very much."*

Kaitlin (standing),
her sister, Molly and Dewayne
Christmas 2000

Danny helps Dewayne with his scooter.

A Note From the Author

Oh, how wonderful God has been to my family and I! He's so lovely and I'm so blessed!

My husband and I continue to minister to those in need. Molly and Kaitlin are doing extremely well and their mother is making progress on her journey to emotional wholeness. Dewayne is now back with his mother and doing well.

Danny and I are working towards opening a home for hurting children, where the unconditional love of Jesus will be demonstrated. A place, where hope grows and lives are forever changed.

Just today, I learned of a mother who has a terminal illness. Unless the Lord miraculously heals her she doesn't have long to live. She is looking for a loving home for her two children. She has no place for them to go. We'd love to open our arms to them, but we need a larger place. If you'd like to partner with us in reaching out to hurting children, please fill out the following form and mail it to us. Also, would you please join with us in praying for this vision come about?

Our message is simple: "Jesus loves you just the way you are and so do we."

Jesus loved me, while I was steeped in sin and rescued me from a life of sin, loneliness, rejection and pain. It's only because of His wonderful, healing love that I'm so very happy.

Jesus is my friend and the love of my life. It is in His presence that I'm renewed and filled with His love. Out of that lovely place, I'm able to love others.

And that is true beauty, my friend.

When Jesus was asked what the greatest
commandment was He answered,
*"You shall **love** the Lord your God with all your heart,*
And with all your soul, and with all your mind.
This is the great and foremost commandment.
*The second is like it, you shall **love** your neighbor as yourself."*
Matthew 22:37-39

Harvest Home, Inc.
People ❤ Helping ❤ People

Harvest Home believes a difference can be made in the lives of people by practical deeds of kindness. Specifically, with the supplying of food, clothing, and shelter to those in need.

The core of our vision is to touch the lives of troubled, lonely, impoverished, hurting men, women and children.

We are currently raising the funds to build a home for hurting, desperate children. These children will live in peace and safety, while receiving the support and love necessary to enable them to grow into well-adjusted, productive individuals. These objectives will be met through:

➢ The unconditional love and power of God
➢ Educational support & training
➢ Family participation
➢ Counseling
➢ Recreation

This home will be a place where shattered lives and lost dreams are healed and redeemed.

Ministry Support

Please Help Us Support the Hurting and those in Need by Sending a Tax Deductible Gift.

Mail to: **Harvest Home**
PMB 177
12905 S. 71 Hwy.
Grandview, MO 64030 USA

Credit Card Donations Accepted By Phone: 816-522-9011

Harvest Home, Inc. Is A Not For Profit 501 C (3)

All Donations Are Tax Deductible.

Visit our website at: www.harvesthome.org

e-mail: harvesthome@juno.com

BOOK ORDER FORM

Blessed Are the Poor
By Rhonda Cahoun

Quantity	
Price	$10.95 USD
Postage & Handling ($2.00 Minimum) Add 10%	
Orders Outside USA & Canada (For Postage & Handling) Add 20%	
Total Enclosed US Funds Only	

Name (Please Print)

Street Number/Street Name

City   State/Province

Zip/Postal Code   Country

Include This Order Form With payment & Mail to:
  Heart Publishing
  PMB 177
  12905 S. 71 Hwy.
  Grandview, MO 64030 USA

Master Card & VISA Orders: 816-522-9011
For Quantity Discounts: 816-522-9011
Visit our website: www.harvesthome.org

"'Blessed Are the Poor' is a book that challenges its readers to look beyond their comfort zones and into the lives of those who are poor financially, yet, so often are rich in faith. The unconditional love of Jesus permeates each story and ignites a desire to reach out to those in need. You will be moved with compassion as you see God's heart for the poor so clearly demonstrated in the pages of this book."

— Mike Bickle, Director,
International House of Prayer of Kansas City

"How long has it been since you shed some tears? Do you want your life to be filled with compassion? If so, I guarantee that your heart will melt when you read this piercing, true-to-life book by my friend Rhonda Calhoun. A warning label should be placed on this book-'Dangerous Material for Passive Christians.' Read this book and you will be changed!"

— Jim W. Goll, Founder,
Ministry to the Nations

"Rhonda Calhoun has lived and worked among the poor most of her life. Her book takes us on a journey of inspiration and encouragement as she opens doors for us to walk into the lives of those touched by the richness of God in the midst of their poverty.

That richness brings new beginnings and hope. Read on-perhaps you will experience that same miracle power as well."

— Floyd McClung, Senior Pastor,
Metro Christian Fellowship, Kansas City

"When you read this book, you aren't just reading theory. These pages are filled with real life encounters that Rhonda and her husband, Danny, have lived. I believe the Lord has raised up Rhonda to become a voice for the poor, for those whose voices haven't yet been heard. "Blessed Are the Poor" taps into that place inside all believers where the heart of Christ longs to reach them. It's a powerful book that will inspire you to make a difference in the lives of people who are in need. It's a must read for those who want to know effective, simple ways of expressing unconditional love to the broken, poor and oppressed."

— Stacey Campbell, Cofounder,
Revival Now Ministries, British Columbia, Canada

"A lot of books describe the importance of living close to God. "Blessed Are the Poor" is a book about real people living in the midst of extreme poverty and in that place, experiencing the concrete and surrounding love of a heavenly Father who more than anything loves to embrace the poor and needy. In that way, He demonstrates His love on earth just as it is in heaven."

— Kari Foss, Director of Intercession,
Oslo, Norway